Contents

Ideology and Division

Understanding the Political Climate and Why Society is Divided

PART 1

S. D. Smith Ph.D

Introduction

Divisions within populations, is not unique to the Western world; and there are severe divisions within nations on a global scale. It is fair to say though, that a unique kind of political and ideological division has gradually emerged in the 'West', and has become characteristic of the political landscape. This division has accelerated rapidly in the last few decades, and continues to develop at a startling pace. This acceleration has now reached a kind of terminal point, that can only lead to a kind of rupture - or significant upheaval of some sort. Understanding what this divisional rupture is, how it came about, and where it is headed - is central to this book

It should be firstly noted though; that 'division' is not, in and of itself, a 'bad' thing. When this concept surfaces (when, for instance, the media talks about political division), it is presented as an automatic negative, and an inherent and obvious bad. Political and ideological division is just a fact - a reality - that reflects a separating or pulling apart: and in many senses, this separation is necessary. A lot of the individuals or groups that lament and decry divisions amongst peoples, are actually part of the structure that has helped engineer, or create division in the first place. 'Divide-and-conquer' is an age-old political and ideological strategy: and this strategy is no less exploited now, than at any point in human history. Talk of 'reuniting' an ideologically divided people, is nearly always a distraction in itself; and is incapable of yielding any material results.

Apart from the question of intentionally engineered division(s) however, we should also recognize that the idea of a political 'democracy' is, to begin with, premised upon the idea of an ideologically and politically non-unified people. It is wholly unreasonable to expect (at least in the contemporary world) a totally ideologically and politically unified nation or people (and the idea of 'majority rule' is supposed to, in principle, guarantee the most equitable and fair system possible). In a significant number of 'democratic' countries however, we have reached the point of *total division*; by which we mean a structure where political divisions are almost 50/50. This is not always the case, and there are nations where either side of the divide has a larger majority. Even in cases where the margin of division is not very tight however, the reality of these divisions is still experienced as a massive strain.

The significance and consequences of these political and ideological divisions, is greater now, than at any point in living memory - and again, there is no working back from this division to a kind of re-unification. The rationale for this position will become clear as we progress, but it is important that we do not start our investigation here with some romantic and unrealistic concept of 'reunifying' divided populations. It is also important to recognize, that a major pattern of ideological divisions - as we now observe them - is their tendency toward *consolidation*. By this we mean that ideological and political divisions become more *oppositional and dualistic*; so that the concept of *war*, or *warfare*, becomes more and more real, at the ideological and political level. Although divisions can be multiple, and across different areas; a defining feature of our ideological and political reality, is that these divisions ultimately find expression as being on *one side* of the divide – consolidated and against, the *other side* of the divide. Even in cases where the political and ideological belief, or value set, is different from the more typical belief set; this ideology still finds its place, inexorably, on one side of the divide, against the other side of the divide - and this is just an expression of true ideological *polarization*.

To realistically use the term *war*, or *warfare*, however; both sides of a divide have to be *engaged* in battle, and using strategy and methods appropriate to (ideological) warfare. Up until fairly recently, what we had was really just an ideological consolidation and 'establishment', that was becoming more and more absolute - with fairly minimal oppositional resistance. We will discuss this more in due course, but suffice to say that it is only through both sides of the ideological divide being actively engaged, that we can realistically talk about ideological warfare, and the use of warfare strategies (and the severe increase in tension and hostilities is already testament to this current state). Ideological warfare is typically 'cold' (in the sense that there is little physical battle); but it is entirely possible that - as tensions and hostilities go 'unresolved' - a 'hot', or physical form of warfare will evolve (that first finds expression in mass civil unrest).

Just recognizing the reality of massive ideological and political divisions — and the ideological warfare that inevitably ensues from this - is an important starting point. Most people at this stage - at least intuitively - understand that this is our current reality, and that this division grows more and more extreme at a very rapid pace. Because the *cause* of these divisions is obscured however (mostly on purpose), there is still a large scale failure to comprehend the true nature of our political climate and its divisions. In this case, knowledge and understanding is essential: and if we can expose the root and *cause* of our current political upheaval, and the divisions that are everywhere present - then we gain much greater clarity as to what we currently face, and what the short-to-medium-term future holds. Being able to anticipate future events, in many respects, simply comes from an accurate and informed understanding of *cause and effect*; so that certain events, or phenomena, follow as a matter of necessity. Another way of saying this, is that we must seize hold of the *zeitgeist* - or 'spirit of the age' - in order to comprehend and anticipate our political situation and its dynamic. If we fail to read the zeitgeist - and fail to understand the true cause of our political situation and our divisions - then we are more likely to be players in someone else's game, rather than shapers of our own destiny.

Chapter 1

Ideological and Political Divisions

Division and its uses

As far as political divisions go, there are a number of classifications, or dichotomies, that we often come across. One of the most popular and ubiquitous ones, is the division between 'left' and 'right'; and another popular one is between 'liberal and conservative'. A more recent one, that has gained popularity and traction, is between 'Globalist and Nationalist': and it is not unreasonable to expect that different terms will develop and become popular over time. Terminology is essential, because debate and analysis cannot occur without it: and we want to make sure that the terms we are using, conceptually correspond with their use in actual (real world) political debate and discussion. We can at least acknowledge that these categories/dichotomies *do* have a place in real world political debate; even if we recognize that the usage of these categories is problematic.

In addition to this 'problematic' status, there are also theories (and individuals) that reject all of these dichotomies and categories as fundamentally false (or misguided) to begin with. The rationale for rejecting these political/ideological schemas as false or misguided, is typically to do with the idea that these divisions and their categories, are actually a kind of artificial construct, used for manipulative reasons; and are therefore not legitimate to begin with. The argument here is that societal division is partly (or largely) *caused* by this form of categorization and demarcation (as opposed to being merely a reflection of it); and that this is not accidental, but intentionally conducted by special interest groups (or individuals) who want to divide the populations by artificially forcing them into these (false) categories, and then use these divisions to make unity impossible. There is certainly something to say for this argument, and there a sense in which this is true (we will discuss this later); although by itself, it is not the whole story.

It is important to recognize that our political and ideological divisions, as they exist within populations; is real, and not some sort of 'illusion' that can be overcome by seeing it as an illusion. It is not only real, but it is consolidating and strengthening on a continuous basis, and will continue to do so. It is caused by severe, actual division amongst peoples - and as this division increases and accelerates (as it is now), the political and societal status quo shifts along with it. The times we live in become 'interesting'; and the events and routines that were otherwise quite predictable and anodyne, are now filled with extreme anticipation, tension and zeal. Where a political loss used to be a minor upset in the day-to-day of things, it is now experienced as a total devastation -

and as a kind of existential upheaval that can have acute psychological effects on the individual. The political and ideological landscape begins more and more to reflect a state of warfare, and the net result is a state of increased social tension, mistrust, division and anxiety.

This increase in division creates new paradigms and patterns. Fundamentally it brings more people into the political/ideological fray[1]: and this is typically reflected in an increase in voter turnout. It is also reflected in increased political participation as such, and an increase in political and activist groups (with a corresponding increase in the financial funding of these groups). Significantly, and as would be expected, it also reflects as a rupture within the traditional political system, and in a disturbance to the function of the 'two-party-state' - wherever that has become the established norm. The 'two-party-state', as it has existed for decades in many nations, is no longer able to function in the same way, largely because it was rarely a reflection of real ideological division to begin with[2].

---

[1] Conversely, the amount of tension and anxiety in this new political upheaval, will cause a certain amount of individuals to remove themselves from political issues and discussion altogether.

[2] In certain countries we have seen the creation of new parties and the collapse/downfall of established political parties and platforms. We have also seen voter share be distributed across multiple parties, that then gain influence and political placement (often within coalitions). A notable exception here is the United States, where the two-party, Democrat-Republican system, is absolute. Although this two party system remains immune to disruption by any potential

Division can also be good for business, and for those able and willing to capitalize upon it. In general, it can be very beneficial for the 'news media' as an industry, that is able to capitalize not only financially, but ideologically - insofar as all of the drama and narratives are filtered through them. New media set-ups are also in a position to capitalize on those seeking information from alternative, less centralized sources. Interestingly though, although mainstream media players stand to benefit from the new ideological divide, they are also at extreme risk from losing relevance, credibility, viewers and capital. We will discuss this more later, but this is largely to do with the internal tensions between needing to be an unbiased, impartial source of information, and being an ideologically partisan (biased), political and ideological *function*. Ideological warfare, as it develops within society at large, will also be very visible within the media sector itself, and in a certain demise of the structures they prospered within, and helped create. Apart from a battle for ratings, visibility and financial share - there is also the battle for narratives: and a growing, alternative media

---

third party/group, the disturbance actually just manifests within the two-party structure itself. Where the features that used to demarcate one party from another used to be relatively superficial and surface, they gradually (and then quite rapidly) became more severe; so that 'partisan politics' became the norm. It is unclear if any break away movement, or effort, will ever break down the barrier of U.S. two-party absolutism, although it is possible that some 'independent', or outside force, could gain relatively swift and sudden traction, based upon the broader rupture within the established political paradigm in general.

sector, threatens the mainstream monopoly on narratives - which is the one thing established media structures fear losing the most.

Media entities are the not the only groups able to exploit the marketplace of division however; and a politician can run a whole campaign off societal division, without any real policy structures or vision. Knowing how to pull the right strings with disaffected groups, is often sufficient to gain prominence and position: and paying lip-service to the right 'ideas' is often the best strategy for political traction. This certainly lends some weight to the idea that the political division we see around us is actually just a ruse to start with, that is engineered by design, as a form of control (a divide-and-conquer strategy). However, whilst we acknowledge that there is certainly truth to this idea; we also recognize that ideological division has its roots in radical divisions amongst the people themselves - independent of super-engineering by interest groups. It is somewhat denigrating and superficial to suggest that *all* divisions, and division as such, is engineered for us totally, in spite of the tremendous amount of social engineering and control[3]. There are so called 'hot-button' issues, where it is impossible to reconcile differences or

---

[3] We should also state that not everything comes down to 'money and power'. It is not uncommon to hear the idea that, if those groups or individuals who engineer division exist, then they do so for reasons of 'money and power'. Whilst of course it is true that power (including financial power) is a significant motive and might in certain cases be the primary motive; the ideological motive and ambition should never be underestimated, and will always be a main driver.

reach compromise; and there is no good reason to expect compromises on these issues to be at any time possible[4]. A politician, or someone looking to be a political player, only has to understand how to ingratiate themselves with the right group(s), and they can reach prominence by exploiting (and then furthering) already existing divisions. As a matter or *Realpolitik*[5], we can expect the reality of division amongst peoples to be heavily exploited by political and ideological opportunism: simply because it is an extremely effective strategy.

The net result of our ideological divisions and division politics then, is that most (if not all) aspects of human life, become a kind of ideological battleground. This is certainly true of the linguistic sphere; and it would be foolish in the least, to assume that the linguistic and conceptual terms and categories that political players and media entities operate with, can be taken for granted. Linguistic terms and political concepts are ideological tools in the extreme; largely because they are the means

---

[4] This is to say that a nation or group that is not joined by a kind of strong moral and ideological unity to begin with, is always at risk from an irreconcilable rupture. If we think of the abortion issue for instance, there is no compromise to be had here, and we should not expect the polarization on this issue to be resolved by 'compromise'.

[5] *Realpolitik* simply means a realistic (as opposed to idealistic) approach, or policy, in relation to political affairs. As an analytic concept, it means an understanding and appreciation of the pragmatic nature of the political/ideological situation (or its reality), as opposed to some kind of (false) moralistic or idealistic interpretation. In simpler terms, it simply means a no-nonsense, realistic approach to political affairs and motivations.

of communication in the first place. So at the *very least*, we have to be careful and critical of the terminology as it exists in political discourse and conversation. As political divisions grow stronger and accelerate, the language will become more inflammatory and prone to abuse/corruption. Terms at this point can no longer just be taken for granted: especially when the term is designed to discredit the 'opposition', or the 'other', from the outset; without any rationale given as to why that person or group is discredited. Linguistic categories become corrupted and rendered worthless, just because they acquire a purely rhetorical/ideological function, and lose any analytic or descriptive application.

Political categories and their usefulness

So what is the most useful, or convincing dichotomy, for understanding our current political and ideological division (if any)? Is it even important that we have some water-tight definition? 'Left vs. Right' is certainly problematic, even if people generally understand what is meant by this and their typical role in political conversation/analysis. These categories have been rendered vague and unclear through time: and what was once classed as middle-of-the-road political policy; is now considered extreme, 'problematic' or fringe. This is the problem of the 'Overton Window', and an issue with categories that shift and have become fluid (as opposed to universally fixed)[6]. However, if we are going to use terms and categories in useful and meaningful ways (and we want to do this), there has to be some norms, or criteria, that *anchor* these terms and their practical usage.

In many senses, the conversation as it takes place in the real world (real world discourse) does guide us; so that despite the complexity any proposed categorization raises, in actual conversation and understanding, the terms 'left' and 'right', do have a relatively consistent function (even if sometimes there is a total failure of communication). 'Consistent' does not mean non-problematic, but just means that we find *patterns* when these terms are used - and this in itself is useful in helping us understand political terminology and discourse. On the most straightforward political spectrum, the scale runs from the furthest side of 'left', to the furthest side of 'right'; and the middle region, is of course, the 'centre'. So it is not uncommon to hear terms like 'centre-left', 'centre-right', 'moderate-left', 'moderate-right', 'far-left' and 'far-right', etc. These terms are the most pervasive in terms of political party alignment, and how political parties are presented to us (to the public). It is also very

---

[6] The Overton window is also known as a 'window of discourse', and is a range of what is framed as, acceptable (or conventional) opinions and policy. What is framed as acceptable or conventional (what is within the 'window') contrasts with what is unacceptable, non-conventional and extreme (what exists outside of this 'window'). The window of acceptability or conventionality is relatively narrow, but susceptible to change with time.

common to refer to - or hear an individual referred to - in terms of their 'left/right' political or ideological affiliation[7].

Almost as pervasive as the 'left-right' dichotomy, is the 'liberal-conservative' one: and it is not at all uncommon to hear someone, or some group, referred to as 'liberal' or 'conservative'. Again, the same problems arise here regarding the Overton window, and fact these terms are historically fluid: and we cannot just fall back onto them in hope they will rescue us from the problems inherent to the 'left-right' distinction. Admittedly, it is somewhat less easy to be fluid with categorization here, because the term 'conservative' contains its meaning and implications within the term itself − i.e. conservative means to 'conserve' (preserve/protect). Nevertheless the term has become a floating one; and the term 'liberal' is itself very problematic - partly because of the origin of the usage of that term (its roots in 'classical liberalism'), and because of how this term has shifted over time.

We can already anticipate a pattern that starts to emerge from this kind of analysis then, which is that we end up going around in circles pulling apart these terms and their legitimacy/validity, only to end up more confused than

---

[7] These terms are also prone to *ideological weaponization*, where they are used purely for the sake of discrediting, or demonizing, whichever group, individual, position or policy, needs to be demonized or discredited. Bearing this in mind is important in understanding why someone might be skeptical of these categories and their usage.

when we started out. It would be a mistake however, to obsess on the historical function of these terms - or the extent to which they hold up under tight theoretical pressure - as opposed to focusing on their *actual* usage in conversation. 'Left-right' and 'liberal-conservative', are problematic at a number of levels: but it is important to observe *how* these terms function in practice. This is because their *usage*, in many respects, reflects their *actual* function and meaning within political discourse/conversation: even if at a theoretical level we find multiple tensions and problems. Most people, even those minimally involved in political discourse, generally understand what is meant by the use of 'liberal'/'conservative' and 'left'/'right': and these dichotomies do function with communicative efficacy in actual conversation and political/ideological debate. When people hear these terms, they typically understand what is meant, and what kind of individual/group/belief-set they are supposed to reference. It is also inherent to the debate itself, that people will discuss the usefulness and validity of the terms themselves; and criticism and skepticism with regard to terminology, is a useful and essential part of political discourse (and over time, certain terms or categories may be rejected in favor of more useful ones).

Just saying that we can trust the real world activity of political discourse and conversation however, is not quite enough. Although observing *how* categories function in actual debate is crucial; we have to have some kind of *measure* whereby categories become relatively fixed and useful (and can be used in analysis). This is to say we need some *measure of testability*; where we look for *constants*, or staple features, that are necessarily present to the category in question (so that these categories have legitimate application) - and without this, political discourse and *analysis* will be an extremely difficult, if not hopeless, task. For each category, the *constants,* where discovered, should not be absent in totality (and even partially), if the category is going to have legitimate *application*. In the social domain for instance, a social 'liberal', will, most of the time, be pro-LGBT, pro-abortion-on-demand and pro-immigration. A social 'conservative' will, most of the time, be significantly anti-LGBT, anti-abortion-on-demand and - if not outright anti-immigration - will be skeptical, opposed and cautious of, large scale immigration: especially immigration from very different cultures. This is just to say then, that these sides - liberal and conservative - stand in opposition to each other, and this reflects their ideological *division*. If the liberal were to all of a sudden become anti-abortion, anti-LGBT and anti-immigration, then the liberal and general consensus would be that this person is no longer a 'liberal' (and no longer 'left-wing'). Likewise, if a social conservative were to announce themselves as pro-LGBT, Pro-abortion and pro-(large scale) immigration; then there is no way that person would stand in relation to social conservatism, as that term functions both historically, and according to common usage (they would in fact, be labeled a 'liberal').

So as a result of an inbuilt criterion system, political and ideological debate is able to regulate and check itself. This is just to say that people cannot use terms however they choose; and as individuals engaged in discourse, must respect and observe certain constants or rules (norms) - in order for the appropriate categories to function. If someone rejects this categorization (which they are always free to do), then it is up to them to locate themselves within a political/ideological space and according to what conceptual description (category). At bottom, a political or ideological 'category', is a just a concept that describes what that individual (or group) stands for and represents (or at least what they claim to stand for). If something (some behavior or speech act) does not match the criteria for the political category, then that thing will be *rejected* as not belonging to the category - and this is fair enough. It might be put into the opposing category, the 'centre', or elsewhere on the political/ideological axis; and it is not uncommon to see this happen in actual debate, where an individual will be told that some beliefs/value set, actually reflects a different part of the political spectrum, in contrast to what they had presumed[8]. It is up to the parties involved to resolve any disagreement here, but we should not

---

[8] This is how the conceptual framework is kept from total disorder and arbitrariness.

expect that the situation is irresolvable. When it comes down to it, political ideology and location (on a spectrum) is extremely patternistic; and after enough practice it becomes easier to anticipate the full belief and ideological set of an individual, group, or party, based upon their statements and behavior.

Political and ideological dimensions

So far we have talking about political and ideological division as though it exists on a 1-dimensional scale: from liberal-to-conservative, or from left-to-right. This is overly simplistic; and the reader will notice in the paragraph before the last, I made use of the term 'social conservative', as opposed to simply 'conservative'. This is because the term 'conservative' - along with the terms, 'liberal', 'left' and 'right' - can have application across multiple and remote fields. For instance, the terms 'left' and 'right', can apply separately to the social domain *and* to the economic domain. It is entirely possible to be social-right but economic-left, for instance (although this is relatively rare). 'Conservatism' is tricky, because an individual can be economically conservative, but socially liberal. This is invariably the case with libertarians and libertarian philosophies, where the core premise is 'individual liberty', free market capitalism, and the minimal role of the state (a minimal role that effectively guarantees a form of social liberalism). Consequently, just throwing out terms like 'conservative' can be problematic; and we have to bear in mind that a multi-dimensional political axis can allow for left/liberal in one sense, but right/conservative in another[9].

Despite these multi-axis issues however, in day-to-day political discussion and discourse, it is generally fair to state that when any of these terms (left/right, liberal/conservative) are used, their usage is typically social, or, social-economic at the same time[10]. It is only when the conversation becomes quite refined and subtle; that an exclusive economic framework is centered around these terms. It is not always clear cut however, and this is why, for instance, there are increasing and heated arguments on the conservative (right) side of the spectrum, about what 'real conservatism' is. Libertarians for instance, are likely to argue that their form of conservatism is 'true conservatism', whilst more focused social conservatives take issue with this, and see the premise of libertarian individualism (the primacy of

---

[9] This is the framework that informs the U.K. 'Conservative Party' for instance; which, for the most part, is strongly socially liberal with a residual, or minimalistic, economic conservatism. The general lack in understanding of meaningful political terminology, is reflected in the fact that many individuals consider the 'Conservatives' to be authentically socially conservative. They are also not libertarian, and are more socialistic than they typically get credit for.

[10] I.e. a conservative is generally thought of as someone who has a set of 'traditional' moral values based upon the traditions and values of their culture and its norms. A liberal is thought of as someone who sees those norms as 'old-fashioned', malicious, and in need of being discarded in favor of a 'progressive' set of values.

individual liberty without state, or other regulatory interference), as actually just another form of 'liberalism'[11]. The term 'conservative', just by itself, generates a lot of debate because of these ambiguities; and we have to bear this in mind when these political categories are used.

What we have then, is a complex field of political and ideological concepts, where these concepts exist on more than one axis. The terminology is subject to a large degree of verification, reflection and correction; even though we need not become demoralized by this complexity, because we do not need to isolate our subject within a purely abstract, theoretical bubble. By carefully watching, observing and participating in political and ideological debate, we observe the patterns and consistencies (or lack of consistency) that attaches to the usage of terminology. The terminology of 'left-right' and 'liberal-conservative' - despite their historical baggage and conceptual issues - still find a very prominent place in contemporary, day-to-day discourse: and will continue to do so, as long as they pick out certain patterns and ideological characteristics, in a constantly shifting political dynamic.

---

[11] Albeit one they are more comfortable with, insofar as it limits the role of the state.

Globalism Vs. Nationalism, (and 'Populism')

As part of the evolution of political debate, and partly because of a dissatisfaction with existing categories, the dichotomy of 'globalist/nationalist' has emerged; and continues to gain traction. This dichotomy is not necessarily new, but it has become more established and mainstream. Sometimes it is framed as 'trans-nationalism vs. nationalism', sometimes as 'globalism vs. anti-globalism', sometimes as 'nationalism vs. anti-nationalism'; and often enough the term 'populist' crops up in these contexts. The media almost never use the term 'globalist', although they will often use the term 'nationalist'. The aversion to the term 'globalist' however, does not appear to stem from some sense of its conceptual inadequacy, but rather from a desire to avoid this term. As these concepts function in debate; the globalist/nationalist distinction is supposed to mirror - with a fair degree of consistency - the left/right distinction.

Again, it is easy to throw out concepts and categories; but we must apply some measure of testability (or verification) to see if these categories hold water, and can be used with legitimacy and reliability. We do not fall into a totally theoretical tailspin here, but again, use the metric of actual political discourse and behaviors as our guide. If we consider the term 'globalism'; then it is generally true that those on the 'left', who generally identify as 'liberal', will largely be in favor of consolidated power in supra-national or institutional mechanisms (as another form of centralization). This is a political reality, and the consolidation and transfer of power to the supra-national (or trans-national), is central to the globalist/anti-nationalist ambition. As a general rule; the 'left', and 'liberals', are far more in affinity with trans or supra-national entities: just insofar as those entities and institutions are the vehicle for left-wing ideology and power structures to begin with.[12] Because these trans-national entities are overwhelmingly sympathetic to, and drivers of, this particular ideology: the globalist mindset and philosophy naturally coalesces with - and is actually just another expression of - liberalist/left-wing philosophy, ideology and goals[13].

The globalist then (or liberal), will naturally be more supportive of institutions and trans-national entities such as the EU and the UN (and all of its 'organs' and agencies) - and their ability to supersede and coerce national law and protocol (typically via a kind of technocratic

---

[12] An example here would be the EU, which is a form of governance that increases in size and power and gains more and more real power (political, economic and legal) over the nations that are a part of it.

[13] If the globalised trans-nationalist institutions suddenly became more right-wing nationalistic, not only would this be a kind of contradiction (in so far as they would totally jeopardize their power), they would instantly lose the sympathy and energy of their left wing liberalist base and support. There is no real risk of this however; since globalism, by its very nature, has something built into its whole rationale and existential premise, that precludes nationalistic and socially conservative sympathies.

framework or structure)[14]. They tend to favor international policy over national policy, and are more likely to advocate for things like freedom of movement between nations (who cannot independently override this freedom of movement), and absolute international laws and 'rights' that no nation can be exempt from[15]. Globalist ideology in the broadest sense, is *absolutist institutionalisation* without exception - where these institutions (or agencies) are largely functions of what we can call liberalist social structures or policies. This centralized institutionalism is supposed to cement the ideology in the most powerful form possible - so that no nationalism or localism can over-ride it, or even begin to over-ride it. In an ideal scenario, *national* laws and policies, will be more or less totally aligned with globalist *trans-national* law and policy; so that there is little-to-no tension between the nation and the over-structures[16]. If the nation did at some point begin to fight with (or reject)

---

[14] A 'technocracy' is something like a system of 'experts', where policy is enforced and built upon a hierarchy of 'expertise' and bureaucratic regulation. Rejecting certain policies or ideological dictates in a technocracy, is often referred to as: 'not listening to the experts'.

[15] If those 'rights', or protocols - as formulated and enforced by trans-national, institutionalized powers - are not respected or enforced at the national and local level, then we can expect something like heavy sanctions will be implemented. The goal here is not only to put pressure on the national government, but on the citizens of that nation, so that they resent their own government for their worsened situation. As a matter of political strategy, this can be very effective when carefully implemented.

[16] This is often the case, and the most successful and functional form of the globalist structure.

the trans-national policy - particularly any social policy - then the globalist desire and ambition is that the supra-national institutional structure have complete precedent and authority[17].

But what about the 'nationalist'? It is fair to assume that the nationalist will, in significant respects, be antithesis of the globalist - since this is just the logic of the dichotomy between the two opposing ideologies. For instance, the nationalist will generally believe in the absolute sovereignty of the nation; and resents any supra-national, or extra-national imposition into national affairs, sovereignty and decision-making. They do not believe in open-borders or mechanisms for easy (liberal) migration. They also tend to value more their identity as a 'people' and ethnicity - and the historical and ancestral legacy of this; over the idea of a mixed ethnic state or system. In this sense, the nationalist maps more onto the 'conservative' category, insofar as they are more invested in 'conserving' their national heritage (ethnic and cultural) and its norms; so that if someone were to reject most of these things as they were just listed above, there is no meaningful way they could be called a nationalist, and little room for them to justify their conservatism. A nationalist will also typically reject the mega-

---

[17] We do recognise that there are always anomalies, and that there will be cases where there are exceptions to what we have stated. As an overwhelming pattern and tendency however, our observations here are largely the rule; and reflect the ideological polarisation we now witness.

institutionalism and supra-nationalism of the globalist: and part of their identity as a nationalist, will be as an individual opposed to the mega-institutionalism and trans-nationalist centralization that the globalist seeks (just as the identity of the anti-nationalist (globalist) will be their opposition to nationalist or localist autonomy and objectives). The nationalist may not go so far as to totally reject all non-national institutions and agencies; but they do not believe that the role of these institutions should play any major (or even minor) formative role in governmental policy - and certainly not in relation to domestic and local affairs[18].

Even on a fairly cursory glance then, it is certainly fair to say that the terms 'globalist' and 'nationalist' do map on to the left/right, liberal/conservative dichotomies in significant respects (at least as these are used as social predicates, as opposed to economic ones) - and there are good reasons this distinction has surfaced in the contemporary political scene. Again though, because political terms are highly vulnerable to *ideological weaponization* and exploitation (where the terms are used not in a descriptive way, but merely as way to discredit the opposition with an erroneous/manipulative

---

[18] As political and ideological division accelerates, so will the identities and positions of both globalists and anti-globalists (nationalist or localist) become more fixed and sure. Whereas the nationalist might start out not opposing institutions like the UN, the EU, the IMF and the WHO; with the acceleration of ideological polarization and warfare, they will gradually turn against these institutions, and institutionalism as such.

connotation, association or parallel), we have to be careful about their usage and application.

We mentioned before that the term 'populist' is often brought up in the context of 'globalism vs. nationalism'; and 'populism' (a term the media do like to use), is a label usually attached to those of 'nationalistic' (or localist) sympathies[19]. This term as it is used in the mainstream however, almost holds no value whatsoever: and the reason for this is that it is almost entirely manipulative. On the one hand, if populism is supposed to indicate a political or ideological movement or status that is 'popular', then populist is verifiable at both ends of the globalist/nationalist distinction - and not just at one end. We are talking about a terrific political division between opposing factions; and the only way either of these warring sides will be a force, is by being 'popular'. Both sides of the ideological divide can claim millions of adherents; so that in terms of popularity through

---

[19] We mention the term *localism* here, and this term is one reason why I am reluctant to say that globalism vs. nationalism is a satisfactory dichotomy in terms of accurately capturing our political and ideological division (even if the terms themselves do have useful and broad application). Apart from failing to capture various subtleties, it fails to represent the even more localist philosophies, that see the nation-state as itself, too much of a centralized mechanism. We can think of certain libertarian philosophies in the U.S. for instance, to be forms of localism; that are not only highly skeptical of, and hostile to, globalised, supra-national institutions - but are highly skeptical of and hostile to, centralized federal (or nationalized) institutions.

numbers, globalism can just as plausibly be called 'populist liberalism', just as nationalism can be called 'populist conservatism'. The ideological faction that is 'popular' will have power, even if it doesn't at that moment have full political representation. Calling the more popular side 'populist' is redundant; unless something else is meant when this term is used - and this does in fact appear to be the case. 'Populism', as it is used in political debate by mainstream players, is more of a rhetorical term that is used to imply a politics, or ideology, that functions without any *principle(s)*. On a more personal level, the 'populist' is supposed to be a kind of inferior individual (with an inferior politics); because their political values are supposed to be based upon something like an absence of moral principle, a lack of 'education', a lack of intelligence, and a general heavy irrationality (or 'ignorance'). As the terminology is presented via mainstream narratives, the true counterpart of the populist, is supposed to be the *progressive*: and just the terminology of 'progressive' here indicates how misleading and manipulative the terminology is[20].

---

[20] If the reader were to probe someone who was uncritically using the term 'populism', and ask what they meant by this term when they use it, they will find that the individual is almost totally unable to answer (certainly not in any meaningful way). Again, this is because the term is used almost entirely in a manipulative way, and it would be unwise to accept the mainstream usage of 'populism', as though it is a feature of only one side of the political spectrum (and as though those using this term uncritically, have a monopoly on

If we leave the term 'populist' aside for now (now that we have situated that term within a more effective framework), we can enquire into the benefits of the globalist/nationalist (or globalist/localist) distinction, over say, the left/right one. As we have already hinted at, the globalist/nationalist dichotomy captures, in a more satisfactory way, the political and ideological zeitgeist, or dynamic, of our contemporary predicament. 'Left' and 'liberal' by themselves, don't necessarily give us much by way of an indicator that is helpful for understanding the overall political/ideological structure and objective. 'Globalist' gives us this, because it zooms in more closely on the overall ambition and intent of this side of the political spectrum; and in doing so, brings to light the overall institutionalist and trans-nationalist design inherent to this ideology (and allows us to interpret the behaviors and statements of ideological players in this light). It also enables us to understand what someone means when they set themselves against globalism, and claim to be 'anti-globalist' or 'nationalist': and then we have the cluster of features that define what 'nationalism' means; that 'right-wing' or 'conservative' by

---

political integrity). 'Populist', or 'populism' are, it turns out, not useful terms at all; unless they are abstracted somewhat from their mainstream use and put to a more effective (honest) use. This could be done by allowing populism to be applied to all areas of the political spectrum, where we find rationality and reason lacking for instance: or by simply using it to designate popularity through numbers (even though this latter seems a totally redundant use of the term).

themselves might not give us. So these categories are certainly more useful in the current political climate; although we by no means need to reject the other categories (left-right, liberal-conservative etc).

One thing we haven't discussed with regard to this dichotomy however, is the fact that a multi-dimensional political spectrum also has application here. The benefit with the globalist/nationalist (or globalist/localist) dichotomy however, is that it is generally true that the globalist will be consistent in their adherence to both globalism as a regulator and driver of *social* policy, and as a regulator and driver of *economic* policy. It is possible, in principle, for someone to be a localist in certain aspects (for instance, buying local food and produce as a matter of localist environmentalism), but a globalist in most other respects - and in fact this does occur with most 'green' movements and green party policies where they exist. This is where the overall ideological core is globalist, and where the localist aspects are not enough to render this ideology 'localist', in any strong or meaningful sense. In the environmentalist case, the ideology is still going to be primarily globalistic, since nine times out of ten, the party (or individuals) will strongly advocate for globalistic 'solutions' to environmental issues more generally; in addition to seeking the globalised trans-nationalism that liberalism typically seeks and desires[21]. Likewise, in the case of the nationalist, it is in principle possible for someone to be an 'economic nationalist' - which usually indicates a degree of support for 'protectionist measures' and national economic self-reliance - whilst rejecting the broader social and cultural ambitions of nationalism. Again though, although these subtleties and anomalies persist, it is generally going to be the case that the nationalist and the globalist is pretty consistent in being nationalist and globalist across the board[22].

---

[21] Hence why green parties are nearly always left-wing, and are naturally allied with liberalist political parties.

[22] Some theorists, or media pundits, talk about 'the death of globalism', because they see the economic globalist model starting to collapse in many respects. This is actually misguided and a misrepresentation of the terminology; since 'globalism', as that term mostly functions, is not primarily an economic concept, but a *socio-ideological* concept. Of course, it is economic as well, and as discussed, the 'globalist' is generally consistent in believing in large supra-governmental functions and institutions, and a large centralized national government that is subservient to these supra-governmental structures and institutions (and all the 'rights', dictates and policies that come with them) - along with globalised economic trade and banking systems. Even if the globalised economic structures did partly disappear, globalism proper (or the globalist ambition), by no means would, as long as the core socio-ideological function remained (which economic models tend to mirror in any case).

Socialism and capitalism

There is one more distinction worth discussing before moving on[23], and it is worth discussing because it is ubiquitous, common and historical. This is the distinction between 'socialist' (or 'communist') and 'capitalist'. This distinction obviously has a strong 20th Century flavor, and was heavily rhetorical in the post-WWII era (especially in the U.S.) and has persisted to the present day. In its function, it is supposed to map closely onto the left-right, liberal-conservative dichotomies or categories - and there is sense to this, even if it is not so straight forward. 'Socialist', or 'socialism', is certainly one of the more problematic categories we are likely to come across, partly because these terms and their usage are often ill-defined. The terms as they are used in the United States for instance, is somewhat different from how the terms are used in Europe. In the U.S., 'socialism' is often used to reference a system that is, for the most part,

---

[23] It should be noted, that although we have mainly between referring to an opposition between polarized opposites (left/right, liberal/conservative, globalist/nationalist); there is plenty of division and tension within either side of these ideological divisions themselves. These internal divisions are not necessarily negative, although there might be a lot of anxiety for either side not to be *seen* as divided. These schisms are inevitable, and actually just part of the polarization process - and currently, there are certainly significant divisions on the right side of the political spectrum - especially with reference to the issue of what 'real conservatism' is, or whether conservatism is dead, and something else is needed in its place, etc, etc. Internal divisions will ebb and flow and will become radical enough to separate prior alliances.

economically capitalistic, but that nevertheless has a relatively large degree of social welfare structures and initiatives in place. It is also used to reference a government that plays a big role in things like the ownership and financing of certain sectors and industries, and that uses public finances to finance various projects and programmes (and these things will typically be present in the welfare state anyway). For a libertarian in the U.S., many of the political systems and governments in Europe, are simply 'socialist' - and someone identifying *as* a socialist in the U.S., often references nations like Norway as being 'socialist' for the same reasons. In Europe, on the other hand, 'socialism' is more tied up with the history of nations that were once formally under the control of Soviet structures and power, and that had outright communistic structures embedded at both the economic, political and ideological level (such as the state ownership of all industries and property). Although it may well be the case that one nation is more 'socialistic' than the next one; if the broader free market principles are in place - then the country won't be thought of as being properly 'socialist': unless more socialistic economic policies and forms of control begin to manifest (as is happening in a number of European countries).

Socialism as a category then, has its complexities: even though the category appears to function comfortably and often enough, within regular political conversation. In fact, the more ideologically and politically heated things become - the more common it is to encounter this term.

Moreover, a high volume of individuals are happy to identify with this category, and consider themselves 'socialist' (or at least having strong sympathy with socialism). It nevertheless appears though, that many of the individuals that use this term, do not really understand exactly what it stands for or signifies: and there is a notable inability to define or explain what the term actually stands for. To this extent, it operates a bit like the term 'left'; in the sense that it is often vague, but tends to hover around a cluster of characteristics that make its usage valid. It is probably fair to say that 'socialist' is even more of a confused term than 'left'; and this is why it is worth probing, to see what staple characteristics can be gleaned from its usage.

So what are these characteristics? Insofar as we have stated that 'socialist' has a high degree of alignment with the terms 'left' and 'liberal'; then we can expect the cluster of characteristics that make these terms function, also find application with the 'socialist'. Consequently, it is no surprise to find that - like the left, the liberal, *and* the globalist - the socialist seeks a high degree of institutional centralization; either nationally or trans-nationally (but in an ideal world, both). The centralization of power (in the communist/socialist state) in absolute terms, is obviously a cornerstone of socialist/communist ideology; so at least this is no surprise (even if the formulation of a true centralized socialistic (or outright communist) national government, remains a remote prospect[24]). Historical communism/socialism, was actually far more nationalistic than people are given to realize (and we can just look at how nationalistically protectionist nations like China and North Korea are); whereas the contemporary socialist is certainly more aligned with globalist ambition in seeking a highly consolidated and highly enforced set of rules and regulations - embedded in trans-national laws, 'rights', policies and institutional structures - that national structures and governments will be bound by. The ideal structure for something like this, would, in the case of Europe, be a European Union that has totally consolidated, and has real power and precedent over the nations that are a part of it[25]. In this case it would be possible to regulate all policy, from marriage, to property laws, from the centralized supra-national government downwards; and ultimately construct something like a European Constitution that all nations are compelled to

---

[24] Strictly speaking, Communism - as a long term social and economic project and system that cannot be 'voted out' - is not compatible with democracy at all. That is why democracy and communism are inherently incompatible, and why by 'communism', people really mean some form of institutionalized socialism within a quasi-capitalistic corporate framework.

[25] Both socialist and globalist will invariably support increased governmental roles in things like the education system (the role of the state - or state mandated entities - in determining and controlling syllabi content), and will even seek that this content be ratified at a more trans-national level for the homogenization and standardization of content. They will be relatively consistent in their opposition and hostility to things like private education, religious-educational schools, and home-schooling.

function within. This is like a pyramid structure, with the trans-national (or supra-national) entities, institutions, governments and agencies at the top of the pyramid: and with national governments lower down in this hierarchy (or pyramid), receiving their directives and policy format from above. Local government will be the next tier down in this pyramid, with individuals at the bottom, that support this structure with their compliance. Both the globalist and socialist have a strong interest in seeing such a system manifest, because the ideology is centralized (or top-down) and primary - and becomes enforced to its maximum capacity, from the strength of this trans-national primacy.

So although we have found a major point where the globalist and socialist are allied (and they are typically in alliance), it is at this point that the philosophy of the socialist becomes somewhat shaky: since they appear to be far more allied, and in affinity with, globalist capitalistic ideology (and its corporatocracy), than their own ideology would typically (according to its Marxist basis) allow for. This is something of a paradox, and in principle, the socialist should oppose the globalist and their ambitions with the same intensity that they profess to hate capitalism. In our current political climate however, it is not uncommon to see the 'socialist' strongly supportive of corporate entities that share their left-wing liberalist ambitions (just as they are in affinity with a media system that has a capitalistic-globalist basis and structure). So the question that naturally arises then, is this: Is the globalist actually more of a socialist, or is the socialist more of a globalist?

The answer here is a bit of both; but it is certainly the case that the group, or ideology, that has been willing to sacrifice their philosophy the most, is the socialist. Questioning motives is sometimes risky, but it is true that this sacrifice on behalf of the socialist, is largely opportunistic. At some point, the socialistic-left sacrificed certain principles (at least for the short term), in order to advance other ideological objectives (that they share with the globalist). The opportunism consists in the socialists' (or communists') realization, that the biggest driver and engineer of the social and ideological change that they seek - is corporate power and finance. Nearly all of the social policies that the socialist desires, have been realized and heavily engineered by big corporate power, lobbying and finance. To this end, advocates and drivers of globalist ideology and power structures, understood that they could essentially buy off and placate who should *in principle*, be their natural enemy (the 'socialist'). If there is any irony in all of this, it is never really recognized - except perhaps by the corporate institutional structures that understand that they have leveraged a powerful ideological group ('socialists') against their common enemy.

So for the time being, the socialists are happy to operate as *proxies* for globalist power structures and goals: and so far this has paid off for both sides in the larger ideological battle. It is very much a case of 'my enemies enemy is my friend'; even though this is a risky game on behalf of the globalist system and its players. For financing and advancing an ideological social structure that aligns with left-wing socialist ideology, the corporate globalist system will inevitably expect a payoff: which is that the socialistic-left do not threaten or challenge the corporate establishment and system in any real way. To a large degree the socialist has no interest in really threatening this, insofar as they intuitively understand that the globalist structures that enforce their social ideology, are supported by and have real power by virtue of these globalist players and structures. In this way the socialist no longer puts all their faith in *state* enforced socialism, but put their faith in *corporate* driven socialism. This latter form of socialism is never fully socialistic however, insofar as it supports a kind of capitalistic set-up (even if it is at best, crony-capitalism), that is fundamentally opposed to the Marxist basis of the ideology. So the tensions here run deep, and there is always the strong risk and threat that, even though those corporations engineered and financed the institutionalized super-structures and liberal ideology the socialist seeks, the socialist will rediscover their roots, and the wind suddenly change direction. Whatever the case, it is certain that these tensions will manifest somewhere down the line; and that even though these groups are allied and in strong ideological affinity, this might not always be the case.

The developments and maneuvers of growing socialist sympathies, will then - be interesting to watch. But what about the term 'capitalist'? Is that just supposed to map onto the 'conservative'/'nationalist' categories? In many cases it does, although it is obviously false to state that in all (or even most) cases, the capitalist is a 'conservative' (or 'right-wing'). We have just been discussing globalism as a largely capitalistic (and crony-capitalistic) set-up; and we have seen that globalists are far more aligned with left-wing, liberalist social policy, than any form of conservative social policy. So the term 'capitalist' guarantees nothing; even though we will typically find that the conservative and the nationalist will, for the most part, be capitalistic in terms of economic policy. Even here there are complexities and anomalies however, and it is possible that the nationalist may believe in protectionist and national self-sufficiency measures to such a degree, that they reject the global free-trade economic models that neo-liberalism typically advocates for. The overall value system might still be capitalistic and 'free-trade'; but with restrictions (protectionist measures) that prohibit, say, relying on cheaper foreign labor for production, or cheaper imports of the same product that can be purchased locally (at a higher cost). This model is not 'liberal' (neo-liberal), in the sense that it does not allow total free-reign to economic structures, but restricts them in the interest of the 'group', or nation.

Summary

So just in going through all of these distinctions and categories, we can see how difficult it is to find a point where we can rest and say; 'this is it; this is the right dichotomy to work with'. There are multiple terms and distinctions that we have to navigate across a multi-dimensional political spectrum; and so many anomalies and subtleties that prevent easy definitions. Nevertheless, It would be a mistake to get too hung-up on these anomalies and subtleties, to the detriment of our analysis and progress. It is not necessary to get too hung-up, because our subject is not entirely abstract; but is grounded in the actual, practical, real world sphere of political, cultural and ideological affairs. Of course, there are anomalies and criteria that don't fit straightforwardly; but the current political climate and its category divisions, do betray clear patterns and behaviors. If it didn't, our situation here would be entirely negative; and we would be conceding defeat from the outset, and declaring analysis impossible. This is not the case however; and we recognize that behaviors are essential: and that through observing them critically, and with as much objective integrity as possible - we can validate, correct, or invalidate our categories.

With the major categories/dichotomies that we have discussed then, we have found no category that we have outright rejected. The closest we have come to that, is with the term 'populist'; although we did not reject that term as totally defunct, or useless, but only criticized its usage, where we have found that to be unwarranted or manipulative. Some of our categories we will use more often, and some less so. The left/right distinction will be used far less, because those terms are probably the least helpful due to vagueness - and as we have discussed, there are more useful terms available. Even though the 'left/right' dichotomy is quite possibly the most common form of demarcation in day-to-day political discussion and argumentation (and people generally understand what is signified by either of these terms); it is less precise and useful for analysis. All the terms we have discussed will crop up where their usage seems the most appropriate and relevant - and we will continue to apply scrutiny to the terms we use as we proceed (this is just inherent to the task of analysis). However, it is fair to say that our objective here is not to continually test the water-tightness (or lack of water-tightness) of our terminology; but to find the political and ideological core and structure that gives these terms (and the divisions they reflect), life and usage in the first place.

Chapter 2

The Collapse of an Ideological Paradigm

The growth and peak of 'liberalism'

It is possible to go on at great length and detail about our current political climate, and all of the interesting and disturbing things that are going on right now as part of the broader ideological upheaval. If we fail to understand the *cause* of this upheaval however; all of this talk will be of little use, and we will still be susceptible to rouge interpretations and theories that take us no closer to a real understanding of our situation. It would not be accurate to say there is only one, singular, root cause of our current ideological and political upheaval; but there is such a thing as a *determining cause*. If we wanted to point the single largest determining cause that would guide us in understanding this upheaval, it would be this: liberalist-globalist ideology has *peaked*, and is now in *terminal decline*.

The reader might at this point, be doubting whether such a thing is true. After all, it is not like liberalism, as an ideology or cultural phenomenon, suddenly became non, or even less, present. Liberalist-globalist ideology and structures are as pervasive as ever - and certainly more visible and functional that at any point in its history. Again, we have to make sure what we understand by 'liberalism' here; and what we really mean is the social-liberalism (and globalism) that has been strongly in the ascendency for the last 150 years or so[26]. 100 years marks approximately the end of the Great War (WWI), and it is certainly true that there was a marked shift in the culture after the Great War (the 'Roaring 20's' followed almost immediately after it). If we want to observe and discover the patterns that led to the emergence of our current, primarily secular, socially liberal framework, however: we can certainly trace this back to at least the second half of the 19th Century, and the advent of a societal upheaval, that was beginning to manifest itself in new ways.

Globally, there were many significant changes and events at this time; although the growth of liberal attitudes and

---

[26] Properly speaking, if we wanted to trace the roots of 'liberalism', then we would need to trace this back to the advent of 'classical' liberalism, as it emerged out of the European Enlightenment (and If someone wanted to, they could argue that our contemporary liberalism is just a logical consequence and extension of, 18th Century European Enlightenment philosophies, ideas and ideologies). However, just as the Enlightenment rejected and called into question the norms, philosophies and structures of previous epochs and generations; contemporary liberalism (liberalist-globalism), rejects the moral norms and standards that Enlightenment thinkers and 'radicals' were informed by and lived with (and contemporary liberalist ideology increasingly rejects Enlightenment philosophies and ideas). Rather than go into an extensive analysis of the history of liberalism (which would be an interesting but distracting tangent), it is just important that we understand how liberalism (liberalist-globalist structures and institutionalism), has emerged in the last 150 years or so.

philosophies were initially unique to the 'West', and grew primarily out of European culture. 1890's Britain for instance, is known as the 'naughty 90's', due to the emergence of a new kind of sexual liberalism and attitude in certain cultural circles (complete with a literature and imagery that represented it). Concepts of sexual emancipation and feminist philosophies were just starting to gain larger traction, and were certainly influential to the new energy and new cultural objectives. Late 19th Century Vienna (Austria) is notorious for its cultural upheaval, which was a part of the broader 'fin-de-siècle' ('end of century'), that France, Germany, Britain, Belgium and other European nations all experienced in their own ways. 'Modernism' is another term that crops up in the history of this period, and this is associated with the social, cultural, philosophical and artistic vanguard, that then manifest in various other 'movements' and 'isms' (that broke in significant ways with convention). Just the term 'modernism' by itself describes a period that was breaking with the past, and that was venturing on a new way of life, with new experiments and new norms[27].

---

[27] The 'Decadent Movement', for instance, is one of the more prominent modernist (or fin de siècle) movements; with its experimental philosophies, new artistic methods, sexual liberalism, and general shift away from past paradigms and standards (and is associated with figures like Baudelaire, Rimbaud and Husymans). The advent of 'Nihilism' is also another significant one, that was more of a philosophical and literary theme, that experienced the present and future as a kind of massive rupture with the past (Nietzsche

It was not until several decades later however (and the advent of 'post-modernism'), that it became clear how great of a shift had occurred; and how far reaching these experiments and new philosophies were. Just looking at experimentation in music for instance: the 1950's (and then 60's) brought a radically new style and paradigm into being; accompanied by a solidification and confidence in individualistic, 'rebellious' and liberal attitudes. The sheer contrast of these decades with what was only a few decades earlier, has certainly led to the impression that 'liberalism' came with the 1960's (or at least with the end of WWII); and it is true that a liberal, non-conformist, secular attitude and philosophy, gained massive traction, and became the driving energy, or spirit (zeitgeist) of this time. Although this artistic and cultural outburst was very striking, and a clear and conscious break from historical norms and models; we should not confuse this bursting forth, with the origin of the phenomenon itself - and we recognize the lineage and precedents that enabled such a huge cultural shift and paradigm to become established in the first place.

So there certainly is a clear historical legacy to our current liberal philosophies and mindset; even if our

---

being one of the main philosophical proponents), and to which, there was no going back. The United States absorbed all these new movements, and the modernist spirit, with ease (reflected in architectural styles such as Art Deco and Art Nouveau); largely because the foundation of the U.S. is built upon European Enlightenment philosophy to begin with.

current day 'liberalism' has morphed away from these historical precedents in significant ways. But what about the globalist institutionalized structures, that we have stated accompanies this contemporary attitude and ideology more broadly? Globalistic (or 'international') institutions and super-structures, didn't just emerge suddenly; and there have always been expansive governmental structures built around whatever political or ideological structures existed in a given period[28]. The last 100-150 years saw the emergence of something relatively new and much more encompassing however; and again, the turn of the 20th Century, and the advent and occurrence of WWI and WWII, is significant, and function as landmarks. Both WWI and WWII were major engines for institution formation; with these institutions typically emerging either as a function of the war mechanic itself, or as a 'solution' to the problem of war in the first place. WWI gave birth to major 'international'

---

[28] Matthew Arnold (1822-88), the 19th Century social critic and essayist, in his 'My Countrymen' (1866), touched upon the issue of federalization (or supra-national political structures), which shows the ambition towards mass centralized structures is certainly nothing new. In discussing France he wrote (in the second person): 'She had always a vision of a sort of federation of the States of Europe under the primacy of France.[...] Whoever knocks to pieces a scheme of this sort does the world a service. In antiquity, Roman empire had a scheme of this sort, and much more. The barbarian knocked it to pieces;- honour to the barbarians. In the Middle Ages Frederick the Second had a scheme of this sort. The Papacy knocked to pieces;- honour to the Papacy. In our own century, France had a scheme of this sort. Your fathers knocked it to pieces;- honour to your fathers." (Arnold (2015): 160). See bibliography for details.

institutions; such as the Council on Foreign Relations, the League of Nations and the Permanent Court of International Justice (PCJI): and a number of these institutions were strengthened, consolidated and renamed post-WWII; so that the League of Nations became the United Nations (the UN) and the PCIJ became the International Court of Justice (ICJ) (Itself an 'organ' of the United Nations). WWII by itself, also ushered in a new wave of powerful institutions that largely persist till today, and these include: the World Trade Organization (WTO), the International Monetary Fund (IMF), the World Health Organization (WHO), NATO, and the European Union (the EU)[29].[30]

So institution formation certainly aligns with the patterns we observed in the growth of liberalist ideas and ideologies: especially as they have accelerated over the

---

[29] Again, many of these WWII institutions had precedent under different (smaller) structures and names, but their new consolidation occurred with WWII and its end.

[30] An increased American role in international affairs and policies, along with the ambition to be a global superpower (or at least for certain groups and individuals to be superpowers), is certainly synonymous with a lot of the trans-national institutional formation that occurred. If you look to the formation of most major institutions post-WWI, the American hand in that formation, is pronounced and significant. If someone was very cynical, they might be inclined to the idea that the two World Wars were actually just a mechanism for an America-centered, globalist, institutionalized consolidation of power. Ironically though, the globalist trans-nationalist framework and paradigm that American trans-nationalists were involved in building (a kind of American, corporate, institutionalized globalism), is, in the long run, probably one of the single largest contributors to the collapse of America and its core principles and premise.

last 100-150 years. In fact, if we were to expand the concept of 'modernism', it would be sure to include the spirit, or philosophy, of international (trans-national) institution building. But what about our statement that this liberalist-globalist paradigm and the ideology it embodies has 'peaked'? There are many individuals (primarily those who associate most closely with liberalist-globalist ideology), who are unlikely to accept this as true: and for a long time, and for as long as the current generations have known, liberalism (and the globalist project) seemed to own the future. The assumption has been that our current paradigm, as it has been modeled since the end of WWII, is a kind of inexorable inevitability and termination point. Institutionalist liberal globalist structures and set-ups, appeared to be the right and only way forward (on the 'right side of history'); with competing ideologies very much on the back foot (and, if arising at all, temporary anomalies at best). It is difficult to anticipate, or even believe, that a set-up or system - that has gradually, and with little resistance, become established and normalized - can suddenly enter into a demise, and that the future of this establishment is no longer certain. The institutional and ideological frameworks that have been built, are tremendous structures that are certainly impressive in power and scope; and the idea of 'too-big to fail' is supposed to be true of the paradigm in general.

So we are also not just talking about the peak (and demise) of an ideological mindset here, but are talking about the whole broader structure and set-up that the ideology is *embedded within*. As a matter of political realism; globalist institutionalism in the long run, just becomes a vehicle for liberalist ideology and intent: and the function of institutionalism more generally, becomes an ideological one. Liberalist social/cultural ideas and philosophies, in pursuit of ideological dominance, do not exist in a vacuum, apart from the broader institutional structures they can be embedded within - and these structures (heavily centralized, trans-national super-structures) are the anchoring point for the ideology *in real terms*[31]. Both the ideology and the institutionalism are now *waning forces*; and this is what we mean by the

---

[31] 'Classical liberalism' on the other hand - as it came out of the 18th European Enlightenment - by no means guaranteed globalistic super-structures and institutionalism. It is true that some degree of institutionalism was contained in the political philosophies; and it is fair to say that early indicators of the globalist trajectory were present - such as the formation of the United States of America as a massive federalist structure, and concepts and ambitions such as *Universal* Doctrines of Human Rights. Whatever the exact story, the point here is that the initial (classical) liberalism that emerged with the Enlightenment, had very little anticipation of the globalist structures that would ultimately emerge with our technologically advanced, technocratic, capitalistic corporate system and structures (that has rejected most of the mores and moral norms that were present at the advent of classical liberalism). The case is somewhat similar with the formulation of the United States Constitution, where, due to the norms, technologies and traditions of the period, the 'Founding Fathers' had little anticipation of how anemic the Constitution would be for a future time (even to the point that it is unable to defend itself on its own terms). This latter subject will be discussed more in *Part 2* of this book.

idea that the ideology, and its institutional framework, has peaked.

Interesting times

It is not as though it is possible to put a precise time-stamp on when an ideology or ideological phenomenon peaks[32]. An ideology or socio-cultural paradigm, might reign and develop for a shorter or longer period - and a lot here depends upon the historical contingencies of a given epoch/period. When an ideology does peak though, there occurs a kind of rupture, that initially will not be felt, but will soon enough be experienced as a kind of disturbance. At this point people will become conscious that *something has happened*; even if they cannot quite put their finger on exactly *what* has happened. A verbal manifestation of this is when people speak about 'the end of an era', or about living in 'interesting times'; and it is not uncommon to hear people say this now – that we are living in 'interesting times'. By this is simply meant an era that is interesting because a significant disturbance has occurred, and a synonymous expression for this would be 'dangerous times' (and this is what is usually meant by the term).

---

[32] It is possible to put an approximate date however, and the financial crisis of 2008 is a good general indicator. I also think 2010 is a good rough date.

But why should the times be 'dangerous', and in what sense? Indeed, the term is not inaccurate, and we can cut to the core of the issue and state that the reason 'dangerous' is an apt description, is because the ruling ideology (in this case what we call 'liberalist-globalism') must begin to fight for its survival and continuity in a way it has never had to before. An existential threat and enemy has emerged: a threat which, in the most simple sense, is a *resistance* to this ruling ideology and its structures. Because of this new threat (this new emergence), the ruling ideology has to mobilize all those defense mechanisms that it has built into and around itself, progressively over time. Initially however, these new threats are treat very casually, and with a large degree of oversight. Because the ideology has actually peaked though (even if it does not initially comprehend this), and is no longer on an upward curve; the counter-force - the 'resistance' - must, of necessity, begin to gain traction and ascendancy. Once the liberalist-globalist paradigm does begin to understand and recognize it is truly under siege, a lot of ground has already been lost; and a kind of panic gradually begins to set in. The counter-force (the 'resistance')[33] rapidly begins to gain

---

[33] The use of the term 'resistance' is risky, since in the early stages of an ideology war, both sides of the division may use the term 'resistance', or 'revolution', etc. In fact, the liberalist-globalist faction will typically identify itself with such terms, when in fact, it is very much the 'old-guard', that has to face a new and dynamic emergence. In any case, the use of the term 'resistance', as we are using it here, is to describe the resistance to the liberalist-globalist paradigm and its ideological framework and structures.

more ground based upon its initial gains, and at this stage, the ruling ideological power, along with the super-structures it functions within, has to mobilize proper. By mobilize, we largely means it goes on the defense and the offence; and in fact, the distinction between these two becomes blurred, insofar as they both tend mean the same thing (any offence is actually a form of defense). In any case, it now has to defend itself in earnest; and the very nature of the battle that ensues, guarantees that the times will be not only interesting, but fraught with extreme tension, anxiety, and ultimately, danger.

This battle will necessarily be vicious, protracted and intense. On the one hand, the liberalist-globalist paradigm has to fight for its survival: and on the other hand, work to destroy completely, any resistance or threat that challenges this ruling paradigm and its structures. As it fights, it has to continually face the prospect its own mortality, and deal with the shock that it did not capture the future with minimal opposition and trouble (i.e. that its immortality wasn't a given). To appreciate the degree of this shock (the shock of discovering real resistance and its own potential demise), we only have to appreciate how successfully the liberalist-globalist paradigm has embedded its ideology structurally, since the end of WWII. Ideological conviction is one thing, but having almost total control of the structural framework of basically all major institutions, agencies, industries and entities, is another thing. Again, 'liberalism' and 'globalism' are not just abstract ideological notions; but are real world, fully operational, monolithic structures - where the ideology has become reified in physical and operational terms, in what we can broadly call a 'system'. Mobilizing this 'system', and having to fight hard to both defend itself and re-consolidate its power, is certainly a shock; and something that only a short while ago, was totally unanticipated.

The 'system'

But what do we mean exactly by the term 'system'? This term is slightly abstract and prone to a somewhat conspiratorial overtone. It is not uncommon, especially in pop culture, to hear of someone, or some group (fictional or non-fictional), who are 'fighting against the system': or that someone/or group was 'defeated by the system'. The 'system', when used in this sense, takes on quite a mysterious quality; and although everyone knows what it is meant by this usage of the term, it is usually in a kind of abstract way. Here 'the system' is framed as an entity with a sinister aspect, that is very strong and very powerful, that is always hidden from view, etc. The question is whether there is any real basis for believing there is such a thing as a 'system', or whether it is just a useful trope, or device, for narrative building (in fiction for instance). It would be beyond naïve however, to think that the 'system' - as a kind of power structure - is not really real. Even at just the most pragmatic, realist level;

we have to acknowledge that *any* ideology that has real, operational power and structure, is going to operate *systematically*. In fact this *systematicity* is what will guarantee the propagation, consolidation, and survival of any ideology in the first place: especially if it is going to survive the long-run. So using the term 'system' is actually useful, especially when it is divested of its mystical overtones, and simply used to reference the super-structures that entrench and enforce ideology from a more absolute and secure place of control. We affirm that the 'system' exists, because we recognize the magnitude, power, and reality of the ideology itself; and its structural framework. Further chapters in this book will help understand better the nature and quality of this 'system'; although for now, we just want to focus on the state of this system - given the ideological upheaval and peak that we have mentioned, and this is important: the 'system' is now *fighting for survival.*

This is already evident in what is going on around us; and is the reason we have an intense political climate with extreme division and factionalism. Of course, each country has its own particular situation, and we are largely focused on the Western world[34]; but the evidence

---

[34] Insofar as globalist structures have been imported almost totally globally, and there is significant pressure on nations to conform to this globalist institutional paradigm (most 3rd World countries have a large degree of imported corporatist, banking and institutionalist structures) - then the liberalist-globalist paradigm has *global* significance and implication (even if the 'Western world' is the ground zero of this ideological warfare).

of this battle for survival is visible in the maneuvers and behaviors of the system itself. Again, it is important not to get distracted by the term 'system', as though it is conspiratorial or something. 'The system', is just the structural unity and organization of the ideology at the political and functional level. Because this 'system' (the ideological structural entity) *has* to fight, this means it risks itself in a critical way, and it is this: to fight, it has to *become more visible.*

This 'visibility' just comes with active engagement in ideological and structural warfare. Although the warfare is not physical in a conventional sense, the maneuvers and strategies required for self-defense (and for the re-consolidation of power), guarantee *exposure.* The more intense the warfare becomes, the more risk it has to undertake: and in undertaking this, it becomes even more visible (thus sacrificing a certain *anonymity* it always benefited from). It is actually not that difficult to anticipate and predict what will occur in ideological and structural warfare, even before the fighting reaches its apex, and the system pulls out all stops in self-defense. There are things that are simply inevitable, and it will come as no surprise to find that political arrests/political persecutions, censorship, mass trauma strategies and the institutional ideological bias of mechanisms - that are supposed to be inherently unbiased (such as the judiciary) - become far more prevalent[35]. We will discuss these and other phenomena more in due course; but the point here is that there is an inevitability in these things happening, because it just follows the logic of an established system fighting for survival and mobilizing its defense/offence mechanisms. It would be naïve to believe in any systems' benevolence or forbearance in a situation where it has to fight for its absolutism and established predominance; not least of all a globalistic system bent upon a certain goal. The system *has* to defend itself, and will use any means necessary to do so: so that considerations of ethics and justice become *significantly* less important than the survival of the system itself (that must be protected at all costs).

---

[35] The censorship aspect will be one of the most brazen and clear instances of the system mobilizing to defend itself and the ideology it is structured around. Information and its rapid spread is perhaps the largest threat to this system, and up until very recently it has a had a near total monopoly on all forms and flows of information. Only with the advent of the internet, and a quick social media uptake, it lost control of narratives in a way that was vital. The need to regain control of narratives will itself, be a desperate, visible act; and those opposed to the liberalist-globalist system will be at a degree of risk for a period. The 'whistleblower' will be the biggest fear and bane of this system, and they need to send very clear messages to all would be whistleblowers (and the system will go with intent and vengeance after any whistleblower who does come forward (think of Julian Assange for instance)). The exception here is if the whistleblower is working for, or coming out from, the system itself. In this case the 'whistleblower', will 9 times out of 10, be inauthentic. When this does occur though, it is interesting to watch how protected this 'whistleblower' is, versus a whistleblower who exposes something that jeopardizes or threatens the system itself.

Fear and paralysis

A pattern that we begin to observe then, is that the mechanism of *fear* becomes a key tool of the 'system'; in its battle for survival and power re-consolidation. In truth, these were important tools for building its structures in the first place: but the *stealth* with which they were able to do this in a subtle, quiet and gradual way, is now sacrificed because of the new urgency. Assuming the system will tread lightly, and with measure, is a mistake; and the damage limitation measures will of necessity, be increasingly extreme. The sheer power with which it is able to strike fear into any would be dissenter, is one of its core strengths; and again, as a matter of political realism (*Realpolitik*), this should not come as a surprise. We can expect ideological super-structures, such as our globalist one, to be willing to employ all and every tactic possible, in its ambition to regain power (and then enforce that power in absolute terms). Fear and trauma operations lie very much at the heart of this methodology (as they do top-down control systems in general); and when this is coupled with an *already demoralized* population, this strategy is bound to be effective. By the end of Chapter 4 we will fully understand what is meant by 'demoralization'; but if we just focus on the fear strategy that is represented in political persecution, threat, and censorship: just these alone are able to impact the populace (or group), so that a certain mass complacency (through fear) becomes the norm.

This complacency, and unwillingness to 'rock the boat' amongst the populations at large, is actually a form of *paralysis*. Paralysis is certainly *one of* the central objectives when using fear and trauma strategies; and can be extremely effective as a tool for social engineering, narrative control and an overall shaping of individual and group psyches. Paralysis as a *biological concept*, is when an organisms nervous systems' means of communication is disturbed, disrupted or broken; and paralysis might be temporary or permanent. If we think of this biological paralysis being caused, or induced by, some form of trauma; then by analogy, we can think of the paralysis of the individual or group, as being also induced by a form of trauma (this trauma is just a product of the fear operations we are referring to, and which we will discuss in more detail in later chapters). The difference with this societal paralysis however, is that, unlike the physical trauma of an organism, the individual and populace do not recognize, or understand, that they are actually in a state of paralysis: and this paralysis just becomes a way of life. Anything that is paralyzed, is easy to manipulate and control; and this is why attaining paralysis within the populations at large is so useful.

Despite the extreme effectiveness of fear and paralysis strategies however, there is a huge risk over in over-exploitation (and a resulting decrease in their effectiveness). Interestingly enough, paralysis and fear strategies, once they reach this level of over-exploitation, accelerate polarization at a faster rate. For an increasing segment of the population - fear, trauma and paralysis strategies - begin to lose their effectiveness; insofar as people begin to recognize and understand what this mechanism really is, and what it is designed for (ideological reconsolidation and absolutism). The other segment of the population however, still remain very affected by these strategies, and become even more paralyzed and fear driven. This latter segment comes to greatly despise and resent the other segment, that is no longer listening to narratives and dictates as they are being mediated via the mainstream (and the technocratic structures this is embedded within); and the already existing divisions between these groups accelerate further (and become very heated). It is a general psychological reality that the more people stand up in opposition to a powerful force, the more people are emboldened to follow suit. People following suit is one of the things the system fears the most - hence the need for fear and paralysis strategies in the first place. These strategies are only so effective however (possibly because they are entirely negative), and the more resistance and push-back the system encounters, the more it feels compelled to accelerate and exploit the same fear and trauma strategies even further[36].

---

[36]Ideological phenomena tends to have an analogue (a kind of mirror counterpart) in some form of physical manifestation. This physical manifestation (the 'event', occurrence, environment), will mirror, at a more symbolic level, the ideological design and intent. If people can be coerced and shaped physically, through some kind of routine,

In over-exploiting its control structures then, the system is compelled to make itself more brazen, and more visible. There is a limit to how much the system can expose itself however, before it completely reveals itself for the hyper-ideological power mechanism that it is (and there rapidly reaches a point where the system does stand more or less naked). At this point not a lot necessarily changes (other than an increased public awareness of the political and ideological reality), as long as the 'system' still controls the *narratives*: which, given their institutional absolutism, they can do for a lengthy period (even after the ideological paradigm has peaked)[37]. The systems need to keep control of narratives is *absolutely central*; and a kind of nexus around which all operations flow and are anchored in. Maintaining this requires the bold and risky strategies already discussed; and this where the concept of a downward-spiral comes in. What we are witnessing now, and will continue to witness, is *the death-spiral* of the liberalist-globalist paradigm. This is where the *very actions* the liberalist-globalist system uses to try to rescue and defend itself, will themselves *accelerate its decline*: so that the *cause* of this downward spiral is contained *within the actions of*

---

ritual, sign-structure or apparatus of sorts, then they can be coerced at the mental and psychological levels. Refusal to be coerced at the physical level will be punished in various ways, until the group or individual concede to being coerced. Obviously, the control of language and what concepts can (or cannot) be used is an instance of this, and will be discussed more later.

[37] In Chapter 3, this concept of 'controlling narratives', will be more fully developed.

the ideological structure itself. This is an interesting phenomenon - not just limited to this case, but generally - where the attempt to rescue and re-consolidate waning power and influence, *ends up having the reverse effect.* This is the death-spiral, and in the political and ideological sphere, this happens when some ideological or cultural state (or phenomenon) no longer has an steady and upward (or even linear) trajectory of acceptance or uptake by the population[38]; and can no longer guarantee the control that came with that consistent trajectory[39].

Ideological warfare

So it comes as no surprise then, that individuals and populations find themselves under a steady pressure and apprehension, given the quiet (but significant) shift that

---

[38] It is not *just* a matter of numbers here, and what is essential is a kind of movement, or zeitgeist, that carries the ideology forward.

[39] By way of analogy, we can think of a monarch who suddenly finds a rebellion against him or herself, and resorts to damage limitation in increasingly erratic ways: with these actions only isolating and emboldening the opposition even more. The system likewise has to use increasingly desperate and risky strategies in its need to survive: but this over-exploitation, leads to increased ineffectiveness - which leads to further over-exploitation, etc, etc. The end result of this downward spiral is not necessarily a *gradual* fizzing out of structural operations and the ideology it is working to rescue, but is more likely to reach a terminal point that leads to a kind of implosion; with far reaching societal impact. This is why the death spiral signifies, almost just by itself, the advent of dangerous times and a period of upheaval.

has occurred. The sense that things have changed, and that a certain normality has been lost, becomes even more palpable: and a kind of nervous anxiety begins to creep and saturate public (and eventually private) life in general. Even for individuals not involved at the political level, this state of tension filters down and blankets the population at large. It also guarantees that whatever divisions amongst the populations were simmering (or have been progressively engineered), come more into the fore; and these divisions just as a matter of logic, become even more extreme. This division correlates with a shift away from the 'political centre' (or point of political and ideological inertia); and this is a totally predictable occurrence that will manifest when an ideology peaks and begins warring with another. This is the basic premise of political (and ideological) polarization; where polarization is a thinning of the 'centre', and a powerful pulling away from it, to either side of the 'centre'[40]. The rule here is: *the death spiral of a powerful ideology guarantees an ideological polarization; and these are the conditions for a form of ideological and cultural warfare.*

---

[40] The term 'political centre' is very misleading in general, and I am personally inclined to believe that there is no such thing as a 'political centre'. Again, this term is not fixed, and runs into the same problems relating to the Overton window that we already discussed in Chapter 1. For the sake of clarity though, we can just think of the political centre as a position that is not 'neutral', but that shares a cluster of beliefs from multiple political axes that don't stray far from the sphere of 'acceptable opinion'.

On a question of time-scale, it is surprising how quickly a reigning ideology, or system, can lose control and death spiral. Historically we have witnessed this with events like the French and Russian revolutions; and something similar occurred with the European Enlightenment[41]. We have also discussed the emergence of the liberalist-globalist paradigm itself, and the significant shifts that were everywhere evident within just half a century. It would be a mistake however, to suppose that our ideological war will be minor and brief; with a decisive victory coming out quickly at one end. Perhaps on some grand historical time scale, it might be quick enough: but in real time terms of day to day living; this will be a protracted battle. 100 years of institution building in the modern, technological era, is not quickly collapsed: and a 100 years of information control and narrative formation is not easily displaced. It would also be a mistake to assume that this battle will be linear, and that it will be a case of loss-after-loss for the liberalist-globalist system, its structures and its institutions/industries. Just like physical warfare, there are many battles waged on many fronts; and even where one side may win on a particular front, the overall war will wage. Multiple battles being waged on multiple fronts, as part of a broader ideological war, is a major reason for the increase in tension,

---

[41] The French Revolution is a good example of how effective paralysis can be; and that once a kind of auto-paralysis in the aristocratic class and its structures set in, this class, even to the highest levels of the monarch, were unable to resist, and even energetically oppose, the actions that followed.

division, nervous illness, and anxiety - since nearly all aspects of life become infused with an increase in hostility, control and tension.

Not all battles are equal though, and if we think of the 'system' and its structures as a *body* (which it is), then like the human-body, there are lesser and more vital functions. The battles that are likely to be more intense, is where the more vital function is at stake: and this is why the fight for *government* is always going to be amongst one of the most heated and vicious of battles. It is an interesting fact that the 'system', as it currently stands, can lose the power of government and *still* reign control. This is because the government is not the true seat of power; even though it will not be able to sustain the loss of governmental power (across multiple governments) for long (i.e. it can only lose government for a limited time). In the event of the loss of governing powers (which is like the loss of a quite vital organ), the other parts of the body (structures and functions), will mobilize to recover this vital organ (the power of government). The fight for government is just one (major) part in the overall picture however, and it is when the globalist institutions *themselves* come under threat, that the heat of warfare climbs significantly.

The purpose of structural power

One complication in an analysis of this nature, is that nations are all different, and have different political dynamics and realities; so that perhaps we run the risk of speaking too generally given this geo-political diversity. The situation in the USA, is different from that of Europe for instance: and within Europe there are significant differences amongst nations and regions. An advantage we have here, however, is that we are discussing an ideological superstructure with *globalist* intent and import; so that the phenomena we are describing has a very broad, universal application (and we witness this in world affairs and occurrences)[42]. There is actually very little chance that heavily centralized, institutionalist, trans-nationalist structures - that have shared objectives and goals - are *not* going to betray patterns and common behaviors. The significance is in the visibility and ubiquity of these patterns, and the ability of populations to recognize, read and interpret them. There is no doubt that the liberalist-globalist system has transferred and built its ideological intent and character into both regional and trans-regional mechanisms and structures; and the success of globalism has depended upon this.

These constants and patterns however, because of their global ubiquity, become a part of globalism's inherent

---

[42] It is actually rare for something to be totally isolated, and even events like the French Revolution occurred within a larger, more universal, situation.

weakness. It is literally a system that aims at as much *global homogeneity* as possible[43]; and it is inevitable that a point is reached where this globalised homogeneity becomes visible and questionable. Indeed, this is especially true once the ideology has peaked, and it rallies to attain its goal at triple-speed. The previous methodology of implanting ideological structure via a kind of slow-but-steady creep, is no longer sufficient; and a new dogmatism arises, complete with the fear, paralysis and trauma systems referenced earlier. This new method has to rely on a system of force and compulsion; along with an urgency to consolidate power in real terms, as centrally (or top-down) as possible, in governmental and non-governmental structures[44]. The consolidated mechanisms are so essential (especially in the trans-national), because their centralization guarantees the most secure form of power - where they are vulnerable to the least amount of risk and contingency[45]. Without the globalist/supranational

---

[43] This is also for economic reasons, in the sense that a streamlined global economy is easier to control, manipulate and function within.

[44] Where the governmental structures have been lost, there will of course, be the urgency to regain these structures; and a lot of noise and agitation will surround structures they cannot re-capture.

[45] I.e. Institutions are not subject to democratic voting structures and mandates (except in a very roundabout way), and the United Nations for instance, cannot be voted out of power (nor its representatives and leaders be elected via public vote). An event like the United Kingdom leaving the European Union, was simply never meant to happen. Everything came down to the public being given a referendum, which itself, was 'never supposed to happen'. This kind of disturbance to a supra-national, centralized mechanism, is

mechanisms totally cemented and (re)consolidated at the maximum possible level; the 'system' will continue be restless and uneasy: since it is the institutionalized, consolidated, centralized, trans-national structures, that are supposed to immunize them from any potential disruption in the first place[46]. These structures in their totality, are the *locking-mechanism* for liberalist-globalist ideology and its absolutism; and an extremely effective armor and defense mechanism that this ideology lives, is protected by, and thrives within. Significant threats to this system are, from a certain point in its formation, not even supposed to be possible: and this structural unity and reach, is so essential to its propagation; that we can anticipate it would rather risk outright war, than jeopardize this structural core.

So intense ideological warfare is an inevitable fact and expectation: whether this be a prolonged state of cold ideological warfare, or ultimately, manifest in actual civil and global unrest. If the liberalist-globalist system did not believe in its capacity to rescue and reconsolidate itself (in absolute terms), it would not fight with such persistence and intent. After all, just the amount of real power and structure it has, gives it a very good reason for

---

something like a remarkable anomaly and disturbance, that can - through a kind of knock on effect - become a pattern.

[46] Again, centralized power does not just mean government. Corporate mainstream media, and its avenues and channels, is another example of centralized power structures. Often agencies and institutions have 'Centre' at the beginning of the their name.

believing in its capacity to achieve what is necessary. We should also not underestimate its capacity for multiple victories, and a certain amount of re-consolidation; even though we maintain our position that the death-spiral it has entered into, is perpetually downward. The zeitgeist and death-spiral alone, guarantee that its extant form and paradigm is fated to collapse: but there are always ways in which it can rebuild after defeat (or after cutting its losses). It has almost unlimited financial resources; and a very refined and practiced methodology for building and consolidating its structural basis. The only way this ambition and project can be stopped completely, is through a kind of shift of consciousness and understanding in the populations at large; so that it becomes something like a tacit principle and fundament, that globalised, institutionalized super-structures and trans-national centralization (and even excessive national institutionalism), is a no-go. Only with something of this nature, would complete defeat of the globalised system be possible: although it always remains a question mark whether such a politic lies in the medium to long-term future.[47]

---

[47] Even if such a hypothetical scenario were to manifest though, it would not mean that all global (or trans-national) structures and operations would cease to exist: and it would be naïve to think that the rejection of globalization as system of ideological institutionalisation and control, precludes, or prevents inter-national interactions totally. Technologies alone guarantee a large degree of inter-national relations and interaction: and although we can expect a certain degree of regionalism and nationalism with regard to food

Chapter 3

The Function of the 'News Media'

The 'mainstream media' and 'news'

The term 'media' has a broad meaning, and can mean just any information that is presented/directed at us via various means (various 'media'). By the use of the term 'the media' though, it is nearly always used to mean the 'news media' – or those platforms that are engaged in presenting 'news' via various means; whether it be written or verbal. Another term that goes along with the general use of the term 'the media', is that of the 'mainstream media'; since these are the established platforms, or organizations, that have effectively been functioning as 'the media', almost in its entirety, for

---

self-sufficiency and dependence (as well as other industries); it would be extremely improbable that import/export trade relations would altogether cease. Global trade and interactions do not by themselves equal globalism; since globalism in the political and ideological sense of that term, is a system (a super-structure) for enforcing and consolidating political-ideological (and financial) power at the institutional and trans-national level (to the maximum degree possible). It is entirely possible (and historically precedent), that inter-national means of trade (and other interactions) can proliferate and prosper, whilst rejecting liberalist-globalist trans-nationalist super-structures.

decades now. It is only with the fairly recent advent of 'alternative media', that this omnipresence and legacy has lost its relative total monopoly on the delivery of 'news' information. Hence it is still custom, that via the term 'the media', a certain paradigm comes to mind (i.e. the mainstream media); and the idea of this media being 'mainstream' is certainly accurate, insofar as these have been the platforms that have saturated and informed almost every aspect of human life and affairs - not least of all where there are information flows. So when we use the term 'the media' here, we are primarily referring to the mainstream media.

It is extremely difficult to talk about the media in the context of delivering 'news', however, without putting 'news' in inverted commas. This is because it is extremely naïve to believe that the main function of 'the media' is simply the presentation of 'news'. By 'news' in the most common sense, is understood information that pictures, or accurately reports, local, national or world occurrences. In watching or reading the 'news', we are supposed to come closer to understanding both symptom and cause of various occurrences/events. Delivering information that reports non-fictional occurrences, is supposed to be the main rationale behind the existence of news channels in the first place: just as though a mirror was being held-up and clearly and truly portraying what it reflects. In fact though, the presentation of 'news', is not a primary function of the media at all; even if the outward mask of the media is that of a 'news platform'.

In an ideal world, it might well be the case that the function of the media is to present information that reports occurrences and their causal phenomena (the true way in which things are connected); but in reality, the actual, primary function of the media, is a mechanism for *constructing ideological narratives*. This is just to say that the media is, first and foremost - a *function of ideology*.

In spite of how 'controversial' this might sound, in a certain sense, it is just obvious. News media and platforms are often referred to in the same way political parties are referred to; as being 'centre left', 'left wing', 'right wing', 'centre-right', etc[48]. This by itself suggests that the media has an ideological affiliation (and it is sometimes upfront about this); so that even on the face of things, the idea of media objectivity and impartiality is questionable. There are myriad occurrences nationally and internationally all the time; and there are incidents and stories that get no coverage: and incidents and stories that get intense coverage. It is no surprise to see one media channel covering something that is untouched by another. At some level there is a *mediating force* that *decides* what information is to be presented to the public (and in what form, using what kind of language), and there is essential information that the public do not hear about. Information is also presented in a certain *context*,

---

[48] The way these terms are assigned to media platforms are often bogus and inaccurate; but just their usage indicates non-ideological neutrality.

or perhaps *devoid of its context*. This selection and presentation by itself, is fundamentally ideological: especially when we recognize that all these decisions are made by very few people, who are already under the authority and structure of a senior editorship and an executive branch of ownership.

So before even getting into questions of content (the actual information presented), there is a very strong basis for skepticism to the idea that the media is a holding a mirror up to reality, and simply presenting 'news'. Nevertheless, it is still common to hear about 'journalistic standards', and all kind of codes and policies regarding news and journalistic 'integrity' and practice. It is presented as a fact, that the mainstream media across the board, is generally consistent in meeting these codes and standards. In truth, it would be unfair to say all media stories, at all times, are false. There is a myriad of information presented to us all the time, and not all of it is false or devoid of basis in reality. At some level, a degree of factuality must be respected (lest the media forgo themselves totally), even if this respect is shaky at best. A remote occurrence somewhere in the world may be more or less accurately covered; and as a general rule, if the phenomena is detached from ideological import, then we can expect a larger degree of accuracy in the reporting. Because not much *is* detached from ideological import however, the scope for the corruption of information is massive. A natural disaster somewhere on the other side of the globe may be covered accurately enough; but a domestic or local natural disaster is very susceptible to quick politicization, and an ideological battle for narratives.

So factuality can easily be distorted by the *manipulation of context*; even to the point it scarcely retains any factuality at all. There is a huge gap that media outlets and individuals are able to exploit, and have exploited for a long time, that enables them to wear factuality as a cover (or mask) for ideology. When discussing *context*, it is important to understand that the issue here is not so much that the particulars in a 'news' story are factually false (i.e. X event happened); but that the selection (or filtration) process, is engineered for *ideological purposes* to begin with. Again, this is clear with reference to the fact that media outlets that are differentiated by ideology (centre-left, centre-right, etc), report on different stories, and deliver different content. A media platform can also present a story that jars with its overall narrative, by embedding it within a manipulated context (or removed context altogether): so that all though there is a certain 'factual' basis, and it is able to maintain the illusion of responsibly and honestly covering affairs; the overall framework and narrative the information is built within, is heavily ideological and manipulated. With any given event, there are countless other events that surround and inform it; and the inclusion of some and omission of others (or the outright fabrication of content and context based upon speculation, or perhaps, 'anonymous' sources), is a very subtle way of manipulating context. It is much more difficult for the viewer to detect when context has been manipulated in this way, and this is not something itself that can necessarily be 'fact-checked'[49]. As a result there is tremendous scope for manipulating information, just through a subtle manipulation of the context that information is embedded within (or removed from), whilst still being able to wear the mask of objectivity and journalistic integrity.

The idea of media objectivity and impartiality is then - to say the least – very suspicious and doubtable. Interestingly enough though, media companies and organizations are conscious (increasingly so) of issues regarding their own credibility (or lack thereof); and the threat this poses to them as entities. This increased consciousness (and the increased public awareness to media manipulation), creates several dilemmas that mainstream media organizations are compelled to face. The media can no longer rely on its previous modes of operation and status quo; but will have to adapt in accordance with the new ideological upheaval and shifts that come with this. On the one hand, it has to attempt to maintain an illusion of impartiality (non-bias) and 'journalistic integrity'; but on the other hand, it is strongly

---

[49] One of the more recent mainstream media strategies has been to use 'fact-checking' as a cover for their own sleight of hand. This is because they understand how easy it is to embed 'facts' within a manipulated context, in a way maintains a kind of superficial 'factuality'. It is not so common to hear of 'context' checking; and the media are far more reluctant to explore the full scope of context, since this would jeopardize their room for manipulation.

pulled in ideological directions. The mainstream media has always been ideological; but the new ideological warfare guarantees that an element of control that it had typically been used to, is lost. Navigating the new political and ideological climate, whilst trying to maintain the pretence of journalistic impartiality and integrity, is going to be a tough task; simply because the ideological mechanism that the media largely *is*, has to mobilize itself *as* an ideological mechanism (thus making the show of objectivity and non-bias increasingly impossible).

The fate of the media

In following the logic of our last chapter then (Chapter 2), we are in a position to understand and anticipate the fate of the mainstream media somewhat; simply because we better understand the cause of our political/ideological upheaval, and the division that comes with it. All we have to do is apply this logic to the case of the mainstream media, and there is no way that the media is going to be able to continue to maintain business as usual (and we scarcely have to mention that there are already upheavals and disturbances in the media scene, since it is increasingly evident). The mainstream media faces an ever increasing criticism and lack of trust - and its credibility ratings are low[50]. If the mainstream media

---

[50] Not surprisingly, the issue of media trust is also divided along ideological lines. In a recent U.S. based Gallup/Knight Foundation

platforms had not built such a monopoly, were not bankrolled by bailouts, and were not so entrenched; the factors that now threaten it, would normally have contributed to its collapse. It is not that simple however. The mainstream media has one major advantage in this new era of upheaval, where its whole core premise is challenged and doubted, and this advantage is this: *that feature that guarantees it can never be impartial and objective (its ideological function), is also the feature that can save it (at least in the short run).* This is to say that the medias' continued relevance and acceptance, comes

---

survey and report, the following statements were made: "Gallup has documented an erosion of trust in the news media over time. Between 2003 and 2016, the percentage of Americans who said they have a great deal or a fair amount of trust in the media fell from 54% to 32% before recovering somewhat to 41% in 2017 as trust among Democrats rebounded. Consistent with the trend toward declining trust, 69% of U.S. adults in the current survey say their trust in the news media has decreased in the past decade. Just 4% say their trust has increased, while 26% indicate their trust has not changed. Republicans (94%) and political conservatives (95%) are nearly unanimous in saying their trust in the media has decreased in the past decade. However, declining trust is not just confined to the political right — 75% of independents and 66% of moderates indicate they are less trusting than they were 10 years ago. U.S. adults on the left of the political spectrum are less likely to say they have lost trust in the media, but at least four in 10 Democrats (42%) and liberals (46%) say they have done so. Democrats and liberals are about as likely to say their trust in the media has not changed as to say it has decreased." (see bibliography for publication details).

It is no surprise that the 'recovery' in trust is ideological, since 2016 was a quite significant year (the electoral victory of Donald Trump to U.S. President), and at this point there was a rapid ideological acceleration. The fact that this is not really a recovery in 'trust' in the media, but just a matter of ideological needs, is quite obvious.

from the fact it is primarily, a mechanism for constructing *ideological narratives.*

The emerging pattern here then, is that due to a sense of ideological urgency, the need to remain (and appear) ideologically and politically impartial and objective, just starts to fall away; and is replaced with brazen ideological partisanship and narrative building. Again, it is a just a matter of political reality that the media was always ideological in many respects; but it now it sacrifices a more balanced position and the pretence of journalistic impartiality, in favor of purely ideological operations. This reflects the hyper-political times it functions within; and it is no longer able to sustain the pretext of being anything other than what it now becomes - largely because its reader/viewership is now only interested in these ideological narratives. The mainstream media can survive with a degree of presence and relevance; simply because its consumer base is not actually interested in the broader philosophy of objectivity and context (hence the concept of 'post-truth politics'), and has become a hardcore consumer of ideological narratives. There is too much at stake for the ideological reader to even countenance information and ideas that do not fit their worldview, and they will gladly cling too and subsidize platforms that provide ideological comfort and re-enforcement. So these media platforms - that would otherwise collapse on account of totally abandoning their ostensible premise (as objective 'news' platforms) - are able to survive and capitalize upon the increased *demand* and *need* for ideological narratives and 'information'[51].

All of this does not come without a price however; and insofar as media platforms abandon balance and a semblance of objectivity, they begin to experience multiple pressures. This is especially true of platforms that have built their brand, or their image, under the guise of pure objectivity and non-bias. The BBC in the U.K. is a good example, because they are a tax payer and state funded entity that does not have to compete for market space in the way a private company would, and it is (theoretically) without advertising. It is built into the broadcasting and television systems as a permanent public presence; and the price for this absolutism and omnipresence on British TV screens, is of course, the requirement that the BBC remain impartial, accurate and balanced[52]. There are also many 'private' news organizations that, at least on the surface, want to

---

[51] This is not an issue of simple opportunism though, because these media platforms themselves are populated and owned by individuals that embody and support a liberalist-globalist paradigm. So it is very much a case of ideological affinity, and the media channel/platform satisfying the demand that is actually out there. After all, these media platforms are significantly responsible for *creating* the ideological consumer and their world view to begin with; so it is only natural they are going to be able capitalize on this groundwork for further consumption and survival.

[52] It is legally required by Royal Charter to do this.

maintain the pretence of impartiality and non-bias[53]; and that are members of various journalistic organizations and entities that are supposed to guarantee this high degree of journalistic integrity. The ideological strain these organization now experience, puts the long-worn mask of ideological neutrality, under quite intense pressure.

The effect of this strain and ideological imperative, eventually guarantees the increasing demise of even the half-hearted pretence of objectivity and non-bias: simply because it becomes too difficult to maintain this pretence in the face of the new needs and pressures. The mainstream media platforms are embedded and have their function within, the overall 'system' that they are a key part of and have helped build: and it is simply inevitable that they have to mobilize in defense of this system. The consequence of this though, is that they get caught up in the same downward spiral that the liberalist globalist system paradigm in general has entered into, and the same downward acceleration and its logic applies. Although for a certain period (during the heat of ideological warfare), mainstream media platforms can capitalize upon the existing ideological divisions and need/demand for ideological narratives; there is only so much mileage they can get out of this. After the dust settles, the amount of damage that most of the major

---

[53] In a 2016 interview with Variety magazine, the President of CNN, Jeff Zucker, stated that: "I think our air, as opposed to others', is truly fair and balanced,". (See bibliography for details).

platforms will have inflicted upon themselves (and collectively) will be severe (in terms of damaging credibility): and although there will always be the hope that this damage can be walked back, the platforms will most likely, at the very least, be faced with the prospect of radical restructuring (if they are to survive at all). We should also remember that in war, there are winners and losers; and any platform (or individual) that was able to align itself significantly and authentically with the new trajectory (or zeitgeist), will come out on top in the long run (even if there are internal battles within the platforms themselves, and persecutions of various kinds).

So the media is an interesting industry to watch, since it is a major battleground in the overall ideology war: and the strategies employed as part of this warfare, will be visible here, as much as anywhere else; simply because this is where the main battle for narratives is conducted. Whoever controls the narratives, will go a long way to controlling outcomes; and the greatest anxiety on behalf of the system and its super-structures, is losing control of these narratives. Keeping a hold on these narratives is paramount; and there are multiple methods for building effective (ideological) narratives. In the case of ideological warfare, these methodologies will be super-utilized: since - in the case of narrative building within an already existing framework - there are no other methods that could deliver such an effective outcome. This takes us into the realm of tested and effective media strategies

- or - how the media undertakes ideological operations on the public in general.

Media strategies[54]

1: The media as a system of trauma

Insofar as we have argued that the media is a *system* of control (a function of ideological control), then we know that the goal and intent of the media is not to *inform* people about the world of affairs, but to *create* the world of affairs (it is also a means protecting and enforcing institutionalist models of control). This means that the narratives they build are a kind of cipher, or illusion, that is presented to the consumer, and general public, *as though* it were objective reality (the 'news'). This is so effectively done, that most people do not realize the extent to which their conceptual and cognitive framework (what they process as 'reality') is built and contained by this mechanism. The question here is: How is it possible to build a framework of narratives, that can influence populations and their *beliefs* and *behaviors*, consistently?.

---

[54] A critique of the media and its methods is nothing new; and although I am working here with my own analysis and observations in the context of division strategy, I do recognize the important work that has been done in this field, by figures such as Noam Chomsky and John Piliger, etc.

If we step back from the case of media narratives here, and just think about methods and means of control generally; then there is scarcely a more powerful control mechanism than *fear* and *trauma*. If trauma and fear can be instilled on an individual (and children are especially vulnerable here) or a group of individuals; those individuals are more easily controlled and influenced. If you can instill trauma on the population more broadly; then you have set up a structure for shaping and controlling that population by constantly strengthening and re-enforcing that trauma - and this is largely what the mainstream news media is. The media understand the mechanisms of fear and trauma intuitively, and through detailed experience: and they understand how effective these strategies are in delivering actual results. As ideological tension and warfare accelerates (and as the resistance against the liberalist-globalist paradigm grows), the media will exploit this methodology to a maximum degree (i.e. even more than they typically would), with the objective of protecting and maintaining their own power structures - and as a defense of the 'system' more broadly.

Again though, this does not come without risk: and over-exploitation due to desperation becomes a significant factor in the overall death spiral here (where it rapidly becomes obvious to an ever-increasing segment of the population, what these strategies are really designed for). This does not diminish the persistence and presence of these strategies however, and a significant amount of narrative building and delivery continues to be centered and contained within, this trauma strategy framework. The way this works is overall fairly standard, and it amounts to *transferring anxiety* onto the public at large. Whatever the media deems a threat to itself and the system (the media of course being a major arm of the 'system'), has to be rendered a threat of tremendous magnitude to the public/society/morality[55] at large. Anxiety and a sense of imminent threat, are transferred to the object/thing/individual that has become a threat to the system and its media structures, and this object/thing/individual is presented as a danger in and of itself, along with a narrative framework to justify this danger.[56]

In pursuit of this trauma objective, the whole media apparatus is mobilized as part of the operation. Apart from 'news' content, this also means that the overall aesthetic and symbolic format employed as part of the presentational apparatus, also becomes essential: and messages of things like 'danger' and 'emergency' are

---

[55]Of course there are other things that could be added here, like threat to: 'democracy', 'civilization', 'progress', 'world peace/order', etc, etc.

[56] At bottom, the biggest threat to the 'system', is the threat to its globalised institutions and their structural basis, function and unity. The structural function is the means of consolidating and holding power: so that if someone refused to play the linguistic, optics and narrative games the structure depends upon, that person would be a nuisance. If that individual were a major public figure, they would become an instant target, and the trauma strategies would then start to revolve around this individual.

delivered through this (i.e. the use of bold black text with a red graphical framework is common, and the urgency and 'concern' with which the information is being presented). Language and its usage is also essential; and a lot of linguistic tropes and expressions have become so normalized, that hyperbole, dramatization and exaggeration, is scarcely even processed by the viewer as being hyperbolic, dramatized and exaggerated. As the media enter a more advanced stage of damage limitation, their language will also become increasingly *moralistic*; and they will increasingly attach a kind of severe moral danger and panic to those events and individuals that threaten the paradigm and its structures. This is actually a form of role-play (moral role-play), but is an effective strategy that is able to transfer moral as well as existential anxiety onto the population at large[57].

Central to the trauma model is that it does not cease until it gets what it wants. Indeed, this is the whole point of the traumatic experience: and this trauma has to be constant and incessant, as this is just central to trauma infliction in the first place (breaking the individual(s) down). Because the media structures are now fighting for survival, power and presence; the transference of anxiety will become hyper-intense. Only when they get their way,

---

[57] Because the threat is a 'moral' threat, it requires a moral reaction from the public. Obviously, in terms of foreign policy, this strategy is also effective for war engineering and foreign intervention as a 'moral' imperative (i.e. part of the strategy used during the Iraq wars and the Syrian crisis).

do they ease the transference of trauma, for the time being, or on this or that particular subject. This gives the public a strong sense of psychological *relief*: and this becomes a *pattern* that cycles and is in perpetual use. Until the media system gets what it wants via the public (public consensus), it will continue this trauma; and perpetuate the fear and paralysis that comes with trauma strategies (and this process repeats and becomes re-enforced)[58].

Media structures are unable to continue these operations with complete impunity and without consequence however. Over time and usage, segments of the population do become increasingly desensitized to this control strategy - even if they are still unable to accurately articulate the process by which it works. In the more advanced stages of ideological unrest, the typical measure and subtlety with which the media would normally utilize fear and trauma strategies, is abandoned in favor of greater intensity and persistence. Trauma is simply a tool that is too powerful for the media *not* to use; and it remains a popular strategy, coordinated within the larger liberalist-globalist structure, for extreme effectiveness. Also, it is not just about traumatizing the public for any *particular* instance (it is that as well), but about utilizing trauma *as such* (a demoralized population in a constant state of fear and trauma). The fact these

---

[58] I.e. Those that offer the cure, are the same that created the affliction.

methodologies are wearing thin, with an opposition growing more powerful (that does manifest itself electorally), is extremely problematic and troublesome for the globalist system; and it will as a matter of necessity, become more desperate and bold with time. We must also remember that those who operate and support the mainstream media structures, are *themselves* now traumatized by the death spiral of their own ideology and its control-structures. As *they* begin to experience major trauma, they will accelerate their own use of trauma on the populations as much as they can (even beyond getting what they want). Although their infliction of trauma onto the public is typically for ideological and control purposes; at this point, it is also becomes a form of *vengeance and revenge* - for failing to cede all narrative control to the mainstream media and the system at large.[59]

2: The media and 'optics'

One of the most essential operations the media conducts in maintaining its structures, is making sure that the function of 'optics' is kept intact. 'Important' is an

---

[59] This helps us to appreciate why there is a definite sense of increased tension, hostility and anxiety in general; since the public are effectively *spammed* with a constant barrage of traumatic content and messaging. Trauma is more effective when it is delivered in bouts, in a kind of ebb and flow. Again, the temporary release from trauma is processed as a massive relief for the individual/public; and the return of trauma after this relief, is doubly effective.

understatement, considering how absolutely vital and essential this is. 'Optics' is an effective means of narrative control, and a way of controlling the information structures at large. It basically means tightly managing the way things *appear*; in the sense that something can be made to look 'bad' ('bad optics), or look 'good' ('good optics'). It is not just a question of visual appearance, but also has to do with language and overall symbolic import. The media is constantly on the lookout for 'bad optics', as a way of discrediting and delegitimizing individuals, or groups/parties, that they need to be discredited and delegitimized. Conversely, it also looks for 'good optics', where the goal is to display someone/something in a positive light. This is just one of the ways that the media is able to manipulate context; by selecting and omitting the relevant information as part of the optics construct.

It is not as though what is considered 'good optics' and 'bad optics', however, is some metric or standard independent from the media itself (that the media then just exploits). It is more accurate to say that the media *determines* the sphere of optics in the first place (or they *construct* the world of optics). In this sense their control is much larger than it would be if optics were not (at least partly), their creation. Again, the optics construct is a powerful tool in social engineering and narrative building; and it is important to underscore this phenomenon, because media saturation has become so ubiquitous and pervasive, that it is easily overlooked or missed. It is very much a mechanism of control, that does not even register as a form of control in the population at large (at least, not to the degree it should) - and just as the guest panels and contributors on any particular media platform, are from an extremely restricted sphere of ideological range - so is the optics construct a very controlled and restricted arena of 'information' and norms.

Optics then, is a central component in narrative building. If the media want to sell a certain narrative, then it will seek a scenario where that narrative can be enforced; even if this is (and it nearly always is to some degree) a manipulative juxtaposition. Many a political leader and political party have been taken down or stalled solely because of 'bad optics'; and many politicians or figures, have been helped by 'good optics'. Insofar as the media is extremely ideological (or partisan), then the optics mechanism is essential: and public notions of acceptability, or something being 'beyond the pale', has to be perpetually controlled and enforced in an continuous and moralizing way through this mechanism. Evidence of this control function is the perpetual policing of situations to see if any bad optics can be found (engineered) when they need to be leveraged (a phenomenon visible with 'gotcha' questioning); or when something needs to be buried via distraction (or just out-right ignoring). So much political behavior is carefully calculated not to fail the optics test; and politicians and public figures must constantly calculate and calibrate situations, to make sure they never fall foul of 'bad optics'. Just this fact alone, means that the spectrum of possibility (ideological permissiveness) is carefully engineered and controlled. Because of the effectiveness of these optics games; individuals and groups will already - even unconsciously - restrict their speech and behavior; lest it be discovered that some utterance or behavior (that might otherwise be totally trivial) is weaponized against them.

As we would expect then, the optics function aligns with the trauma model in significant respects; and we can anticipate that mechanisms of ideological control will have a high degree of crossover and connectedness. In fact, in order for the optics structures to operate constantly and with maximum effectiveness, they must merge with fear and trauma mechanisms to a large degree. What is deemed 'bad optics' at the political/ideological level, is supposed to reflect badness in general: and the public are supposed to react to this accordingly (a form of moral congruence). So 'optics' becomes a form of social control, whereby people are cognitively shaped and 'morally' engineered by various 'transgressions' and 'taboos' - where these transgressions and taboos might entirely be constructed by the system in general. Transgressions come with consequences; and not only is the political actor controlled by potential transgression, but the public is continually held in check by the optics system and its punishment structures. Such phenomena is not limited to the political sphere, but is evident in places like the corporate sphere as well. It is very much like having to perpetually and carefully navigate a series of traps, lest one fall into one and be permanently maimed. The best way to avoid traps is just to avoid terrain where traps exist; so that individuals, in many cases, due to fear, would rather avoid those areas or domains where the risk of falling foul of optics is high (or just possible to begin with). No one wants to walk into a landmine; and even having to navigate mine littered territory is enough to put off most individuals. This is how powerful the optics system is; and why there is no small level of anxiety transferred onto the public at large, via the omnipresence of the optics structure.

3: The media as an input-output system

Again, this is not something that is totally apart from the other media mechanisms, but it is worth discussing independently. The function of the media as a system in general, is one whereby a certain *input* is given ('information'/data, that is given to the public), in return for a certain *output* (public reaction). The media system is not ego-less or selfless and expecting nothing in return for its input. What is essential, is that the output must be relatively predictable and reliable; and in this sense it is a control system that has to be perpetually functioning. Once the output no longer becomes reliable and consistent, the media system begins to panic; because its operational structures are becoming redundant and ineffective. In order to (attempt) a reconsolidation of narrative control, it has to fall back on the trauma model; and this where there is significant alignment. In accelerating the trauma methodology, the goal is to make the input/output system work like it should: as a reliable system for controlling public reaction, and gaining the compliance that the media need for their ideological operations and structures[60].

With regard to the concept of 'input/output', it is in this sense that the we can legitimately talk about the media as a system of *programming*. Just as in computing, inputting data (code) generates a certain outcome; the mainstream media, in league with broader media in general, operates along the same premise. An individual who responds exactly in the way they are supposed to, in accordance with media narratives, is 'programmed': and the input here works as it is supposed to, in *generating* the output (and guaranteeing a certain outcome). Extrinsic, uncontrolled data, is a threat to the outputs; and hence the reason why the mainstream media are one of the main advocates for censoring, or excluding, alternative, or outside media sources.

---

[60] Or objectives such as foreign intervention, 'spreading democracy' or war engineering (typically to bring a foreign nation under globalist control, as a new node in its globalist structure).

4: Victim politics and division strategy

In the beginning of this book, we stated that although we rejected the idea that division in society is *totally* engineered by certain forces/individuals; it is certainly true that there are intense, persistent and omnipresent individuals/groups that *do*, as a matter of fact, cause societal division (and that this is also done by design, and not by accident). The mainstream media is a prime example of a mechanism, or structure, that creates societal division on a broad scale, as a matter of ideological intent.

Again, an alignment with the trauma model here is natural and necessary – and this is where the issue of *demographics* comes into play. There is a kind of taboo in even talking about this in factual terms; due to the way the subject and scope of this factor has been controlled (as part of the optics game). The strategy here is a simple, but effective one, and has been employed by the media system for a long time with great success. The core operation is this: *to sell the currency of 'victimhood' and 'oppression' to as many 'minority' demographic groups as you can, so that they are an easy political sell.* In other words, if you keep telling people they are the victim of some group *X*, and that in order to get justice, or equality, they need to vote against X and vote Y; that group will, as a general rule, vote for Y.

Although the underlying mechanism here is simple, it cannot be too transparent and obvious. A lot of subterfuge is required; and the media structures must work to maintain the illusion (until they can no longer do so) that all they are doing, is presenting 'news' information to the public. The selection and prioritization of information (and the mass manipulation of context) is, by itself, sufficient to control public perception here: and the media is able to carefully construct narratives over time that reinforce the 'victim' narrative. It is no coincidence for instance, that minority demographic groups throughout the West are totally consistent in voting for left-wing, liberalist-globalist political parties. This is certainly paradoxical in the case of groups who, whilst generally identifying as 'conservative' in religion and life, primarily vote for left-wing liberalist parties.

This is media engineering at its finest, and a show of how effectively they are able to engineer the electorate for ideological control - and sustain the extant power structures. In order to maintain these ideological/power structures, they need a segment of the population that they can engineer and rely upon as their fundament. They also need to increase the population of these 'minority groups'; especially with the advent of the death spiral of the liberalist-globalist paradigm. This segment of the population that is targeted, must be perpetually angry and indignant with what they perceive as the extreme injustice of their social (and economic) situation. The media thrive off these emotions and concepts with carefully structured narratives/information, that they have helped engineer and shape to begin with (and the input/output mechanism here works reliably and consistently)[61]. If by any chance this system starts to fail, the media has to ramp up this victim politics (through a form of trauma induction), so that the 'oppressed' demographic groups (the victims) fall back into place. 'These people hate you', 'these people are your enemies', 'you need to overthrow this hierarchy/system to be free and attain justice', etc, etc; is the text and subtext continually present. These narratives are eagerly consumed by a people whose *whole identity has been collapsed into the identity of victim/the oppressed*: and in doing this, the media foment and create divisions as part of an overall strategy for controlling the electorate and its behavioral patterns[62].

So the division engineered by the media here is certainly not minor, and the reality we face is a political and ideological division that is significantly demarcated along

---

[61] Whilst of course it is true that, in the world, there is no shortage of injustice and wrongs (and real victims); the way the narratives about oppression and injustice are engineered, not only by the media, but by all arms of the liberalist-globalist system, are largely of ideological import and structure, and thereby misleading by design.

[62] The 'victim(s)' are also never in the wrong, and never allowed to be in the wrong. If there is some negative action on their part, the guilt is always transferred to another party. In this way the 'victims' never have to take self-responsibility, and are kept in a permanent state of immaturity (that makes them easier to control).

demographic lines[63]. Again, the ideological framework of a demographic people, will, in many demographics, be largely consistent. In the United States for instance, the African-American community are almost totally consistent in their vote and support of the Democrat party. The same is true (although slightly less so) for the Latino/Hispanic community. Women (especially young women between the ages of 18-25) are far more likely to vote for left-wing, liberalist parties/individuals/policies. In Europe, Australia and America, the Islamic communities are overwhelmingly likely to vote for left-wing parties, policies and individuals; despite the ostensible conservatism of their own religion and philosophies. The same patterns are ubiquitous throughout the West (it is easy to observe them in statistics), and the politics of *identity* are essential to creating these patterns. In many respects, this is one of the biggest guns in the media arsenal; and a key reason they still have so much traction in the first place. It is the age old strategy of divide-and-conquer, and its effective utilization. Engineered demographic warfare (which contains the trauma function), is now a key rallying objective for the maintenance and reconsolidation of diminishing ideological power structures[64].

---

[63] Not totally demographic of course, but voting patterns do betray clear and strong patterns along demographic lines.

[64] Despite this effort, one thing we can nevertheless expect to see is the breakdown of this media strategy. These divide-and-conquer strategies are becoming increasingly transparent to the population at

It is also interesting and worthy of note, that the media employ this same tactic on themselves, and will do this more and more, as their methodology falls under increased scrutiny, resentment and criticism. 'Playing the victim' when in the wrong, is a universal and extremely effective strategy, where guilt is transferred (or attempted to transfer) onto the other, and away from oneself. Of course one might actually be a victim (and we are not denying that there are real victims), but we are here talking about a phenomenon where victimhood is *weaponized* as a tool or strategy. By transferring the wrongdoing onto another, the media engineer a situation whereby they cannot be criticized - and where this criticism or resentment becomes a 'gross injustice' (an 'attack' on the media): so that criticizing or 'attacking' them, becomes 'dangerous' and 'shameful' (a so called 'threat to democracy'). Thus the mainstream, corporate media in the U.S., can often be heard lamenting that the 'free press' (the press being the only industry mentioned in the U.S. Constitution), is 'under attack' and being 'mistreated'. This is absurd in the extreme, not least of all because the 'free press' scarcely exists in the United States to begin with: and the current mainstream media platforms are not a 'free-press', but a heavily controlled

---

large; and a significant number of those demographics that are being engineered with victim/identity politics, are also starting to become conscious of the extent to which they are being used as pawns and proxies. It is also naïve of the media to think that - even if they get away with this mass engineering; these demographic groups will remain subservient and complacent with mainstream media entities.

and heavily controlling, corporate and ideological monopoly. Also, because this same media is an extremely manipulative system of subterfuge (wearing the mask of objectivity and 'public service' (or 'civic duty')), it has little claim to actually fulfilling the role of actual journalism and reportage. Nevertheless, utilizing victimhood is an effective strategy; especially when you still have relatively large control over what narratives circulate.

5. The media and language

There is of course overlap here with the other points, and the overlap makes for some interesting points. The overlap, or affinity with the optics feature, is interesting and topical; because here we encounter the phenomenon of what is commonly known as, 'political correctness'. The concept of 'political correctness' is fairly mainstream now, and most people understand what is meant by this. More often than not, it is used in a critical way to condemn or disapprove of, the excessive policing of language, and the ideas (concepts) that language conveys (and it is not uncommon to find references to 'newspeak' or 'George Orwell' in this context).

But what is the actual function of political correctness? There is no doubt that we are in a period when there is a decisive focus and goal in regulating (or policing) language and concepts; not only in public life, but in the private sphere as well. We could go into detail about what kind of ideology is currently being protected and enforced by political correctness, and what ideologies/ideas are being excluded/rendered non-permissible: but the general and overall function provides sufficient insight into the overall objective and intent (especially in the context of the peak of an ideological paradigm). This function is very much that of the *optics function* in general; which is to say that the intent of political correctness structures, is to create a heavily engineered and controlled environment that determines, 1: what ideological content and ideas are permitted and encouraged (as socially and politically acceptable), and 2: what is not ideologically permitted; and rendered a kind of heresy (or transgression) by the political and ideological structures and norms.

It is not just that a transgression is punished however, or that performing a politically incorrect act is met with social stigma. Whilst it is all of this as well; the broader, more potent function of the 'political correctness' mechanism, is to make it impossible (or unlikely) to even *think* a certain way *in the first place*. The individual mindset and *cognitive structure* is very much formed and shaped by the *linguistic structure* that exists, and that is continually micro-engineered as a mirror and expression of the ideology itself[65]. This is why, ideally, the political

---

[65] This of course ties in with the function of Neuro-Linguistic programming (NLP). NLP is interesting in the political/ideological sphere, but in other domains, may have a primarily pragmatic function. In the corporate domain for instance, corporations use NLP

correctness structures have to be in position with even the earliest stages of human life; so that the individual life is circumscribed by this ideological super-structure and its limits. It is simply inevitable and par for course, that all media structures - from the 'entertainment' industries to the 'news' media industries - will have a *strong interest in children*. Of course, there are purely pragmatic interests that relate to power and profit; but the more encompassing interest is an ideological interest in guaranteeing (trying to guarantee) that the ideological framework makes a lasting and firm imprint on the human mind from the very beginning. This is just what we would expect of an 'input/output' system; where the stake is a reliable and steady population of engineered (programmed) individuals, that will serve as the functional base for the continuance, propagation and survival of the ideology and its super-structures.

The 'programming' allegory then, ceases to be just an allegory; but is an accurate and apt description of the actual ideological function here. For individuals unused to discussion and concepts of this kind, the idea that people are 'programmed' may seem like an exaggeration or overstretch (or at best just an allegory); and no one wants to believe that they are 'programmed', even if it is just to a degree. But this is the process that targets the

---

techniques and programmes as tools for the purpose of maximizing profit, and employee efficiency (and things like group coherence and function). Even this pragmatic function however, is unlikely to be *purely* pragmatic; but will have an ideological role as well.

individual from the earliest years of their lives, and that places them within a sea of ideological content and messaging (that is often not even recognized as ideological). The prize here is nothing less than full ideological sway and influence over the populations; through utilizing the right methodologies, and the available, emerging and popular technologies. The success is largely guaranteed across a significant segment of the population, because the inputs are engineered and designed to deliver the output. The idea of a *tabula-rasa* (the human as a 'blank slate') becomes relevant here; and the individual is programmed from the ground-up, using the super-structure that has been *built around the individual* in its entirety (a structure which, in its fully-consolidated state, the individual has little escape from).

One more linguistic feature worth mentioning before moving on, is the effect of labeling, or concept placement. In advertising, 'brand placement' is where a branded product is subtly (or not so subtly) placed in an environment/setting that will receive a lot of consumer traffic; just like placing a branded soft drink in a popular sitcom, or something like that. Likewise, when the media want to enforce a concept, and make it branch out, they will just start using a term, or set or terms, repeatedly; so that the concept is placed, or situated, into the public domain. This is an *electrification* strategy that *energizes* a term or idea; even if the term or idea is not actually relevant, or proportionate in this instance (or any instance). This 'electrification' circulates the relevant concept(s) and terminology rapidly into the information structures, so that these new terms and ideas are quickly normalized and become topical. Electrification is rarely generated via one source, but is typically generated via multiple media platforms - usually simultaneously - and through a kind of affinity (or coordinated effort). When this current flows through the information structures, and the sphere these structures encompass (almost everything), it has the effect of making the concept urgent and relevant; so that the population are *energized* and wired with this current. This strategy does not always work, and becomes less and less effective with time (largely due to over-exploitation); but it is still a powerful psychological tool and method for normalizing what needs to be normalized, and energizing concepts or ideas that need to be energized. This works through a kind of affirmation and enforcing via linguistic repetition; and when looked at broadly, looks just like a programming structure/mechanic[66]. Conversely, if there is a situation or incident that conflicts with mainstream narratives, the media will downplay and ignore that situation, so as to give it little-to-zero, linguistic traction or significance. In

---

[66] These methods and techniques are utilized in multiple areas, including 'cognitive behavior therapies', as a way of 'reconditioning' the mind to deal with various issues and mental or psychological disturbances or blockades. 'Positivity' strategies also employ a kind of affirmation through repetition and enforcement.

this case, it is a question of non-electrification, and actual measures to prevent electrification (or cut the current)[67].

Summary

There is a lot more we could discuss in this chapter, but our goal has been to keep our focus on understanding ideological mechanisms and strategies; and how they bear upon our current predicament with relation to the collapse of an ideological paradigm (and the political and ideological upheaval (and division) that comes with that). There is no question that the norms and patterns mainstream media networks and platforms were used to operating within (and had helped build), are in a state or disarray and disturbance. This is just to be expected with an institutional set-up that is embedded within a collapsing and unstable paradigm. What is interesting is the way this institution (the mainstream news media) responds and deals with the threat they face. Again, the peak and death spiral of the liberalist-globalist paradigm, is just echoed, or mirrored in, this media death spiral: and rather than adapt towards a long term, more sustainable strategy, they fall back on their tried and tested methods.

---

[67] In continuing this analogy, we can think of individuals (the public) as being like *conductors* for this current; where there have to be a sufficient amount of conductors in the population in order to carry this current (concepts/narratives), and make it circulate sufficiently. The strategies we have discussed are for maintaining this network of receptive individuals (conductors).

These methods, when accelerated and over-exploited, only accelerate the downward spiral at a quickening pace, and lead to further exploitation that uncovers the media for the ideological function that it is.

All of this doesn't mean the mainstream media just disappears however; and it is difficult to anticipate a capitalist technological digital environment where large news media organizations and institutions are not present. What does change though, is the mode, or model, that the mainstream corporate platforms have been used to for a long time. Certain platforms will be able to get a lot of mileage out of just becoming brazen ideological platforms and narrative structures; even though there are limits to how far this can be carried (and how long media platforms can be artificially subsidized and bailed out). In the meantime though, and as ideological warfare continues, all of the above methodologies we discussed, will be ramped up and exploited to their maximum extent; especially the methods that are going to introduce *paralysis and division.* This means that the *trauma model* (as a means of paralysis, control and revenge) and *victim narratives*, will become extremely visible and ubiquitous. Just the constant of trauma, is enough to wear the average citizen down into a state of exhaustion and demoralization; and paralysis makes active opposition increasingly unlikely. The utilization of victim narratives involves *super-activating* the demographic divisions that the media have helped successively engineer over decades; and again, this is a strategy that is really too effective (at least short-term) not to use. This strategy will also be relied heavily upon in proximity to a major election; where emotional energy and injustice narratives can hyper-activate and energize multiple demographic groups simultaneously. Activating divisions that the media have themselves engineered, as part of an overall strategy for ideological control and consolidation, is very much going to be the norm going forward (along with extreme trauma this involves); and it is false in the extreme, to presume that ideological and political divisions will be healed through some effort on behalf of the 'news' media themselves[68].

---

[68] There might be some skepticism to the argument I have outlined in this chapter. After all, what if someone does not watch, read or engage with much mainstream media at all? It would seem that person is free from the influence described above, and that media influence is surely over-exaggerated? It is crucial to understand though, that the way the media systems operate on individuals and the population as a whole, is not primarily, or even necessarily, via establishing *direct* links to people (like a line that goes from the media source to the customer); but by creating *spheres*, that all people are compelled to function and live within. These spheres are like spheres of code, that are primarily invisible: and this coding just corresponds with what we already discussed in this chapter in terms of an input/output system. Of course the 'news' media does not work in isolation when constructing these spheres, or this 'matrix'; and it is in affinity with the ideological institutionalized structures in their totality, that they are more broadly effective. So even if someone is 'apolitical', or not engaged directly and actively with media content; this in no way guarantees that individual is somehow immune to media methodology and influence: since they live within the sphere of code that infects and permeates and *builds* everything within that sphere. This means that practically all cognitive, social and cultural products that exist, grow and develop within the sphere;

are *coded*, or programmed, by these ideological entities: and this is true of even individuals *themselves*, who are born and coded within these spheres. This is how ideology is formed *totally*, by the *engineering of the sphere*. Because we recognize the non-deterministic aspect of the human will however, we will not say that everyone is doomed to be programmed or engineered by the ideological superstructure and its engineers. There is never a guarantee of effectiveness, and there will always remain a segment of the population who resist, or have developed immunity to the programming. These anomalies are always perceived as a threat to the sphere (or matrix), and the objective is not to make sure everyone is programmed (which is impossible), but to make sure that those who are immune to the input/output operations, are rendered powerless against the system (or matrix) in any rebellion they might formulate. Censorship, political imprisonment, persecutions, and paralysis/fear operations; are all just a part of this protecting of the 'matrix' - where the objective is that the sphere not get corrupted, or threatened, with any oppositional code (a kind of counter-code or 'virus'). The ultimate goal is to make even basic resistance impossible: and if anything challenges, or threatens, the overall sphere and its coded content; the system, or matrix, will mobilize its defense systems to *destroy this threat*. Because the sphere is growing weaker and is essentially infected with viral content already, the 'system' and its 'agents' double-down with the intent of reconsolidating power - and we get the ideological warfare, division and other phenomena we have been discussing in this book. Obviously, this phenomenon seems to bear upon the meaning and symbolism in the movie 'The Matrix', and the notion of 'agents' who are coded into the matrix's defense system (at least it is a very plausible reading of this movie). With regard to the notion of a 'sphere'; a more complete concept of 'globalism', is when all the local/regional spheres - that have grown and been coded by the same messaging/code/structures - all begin to *coalesce,* so that there is a *merging of the spheres* into one giant (universal) coded sphere (of course with some remaining regional/local/cultural anomalies and features (although these things become increasingly superficial in the face of increased homogenization)).

Chapter 4

Other Forms of Media and Their Ideological Role

In the last chapter, we discussed the mainstream news media as an extremely prevalent media form, that has a dominant ideological role and function. There are of course, many other forms of media; and in a media saturated epoch, where so much is at stake - politically and ideologically - it would hardly come as a surprise to find that *other forms* of media carry significant ideological baggage. In fact, it would not be worth discussing these other forms of media in this book, if they were not also largely, *functions of ideology*. Because they are significant in this respect, the discussion of these other forms of media, will occupy this chapter.

Advertising media, emotionality, and consumption

It is probably not necessary to construct a hierarchy of which media format has the largest ideological role or function; since the most powerful ideological effect and presence, is when all industries or functions, work together as an input system. Nevertheless, it is true that there are certain industries, or sectors, that have more powerful and reaching roles. The news media we have already discussed, and is obviously a powerful sector in terms of ideological reach and influence: and we will make the argument that entertainment media is also powerful in this respect; and so is advertising media.

Starting with advertising media, it is fair to say this sector is very powerful; if not simply because of its sheer ubiquity, and uncritical and established uptake into almost every arena of human affairs and interactions. This omnipresence and reach makes advertising a key ideological player; and there is little chance that something so ubiquitous and media-rich, would be neglected in this respect. In many ways, advertising is just raw ideological intent and messaging: and this is especially true of advertising in our ideologically saturated, contemporary society (even if we need not say that advertising is inevitably and always, ideologically laden[69]). Even just a casual glance at advertising content suggests its investment in ideological strategy and goals: and insofar as it is ideological (and a function of a specific paradigm), we are able to observe many of the same

---

[69] Of course, advertising as it exists within a capitalist framework, will embody and support capitalistic structures and models. There is, nevertheless, such a thing as advertising that is primarily based upon product promotion/recognition (i.e. someone has a product, and wants to create awareness for that product). If we think of this 'product recognition' as a kind of minimalistic idea of advertising; then it is certainly true that this minimalistic notion is a relatively common one that people stick to when thinking of the central and main purpose of advertising (marketing products for the sake of generating and maximizing profits).

patterns it shares with other ideological functionaries (such as the news media industry).

One major pattern we observe, is the extent to which advertising becomes more flagrantly ideological as the liberalist-globalist paradigm peaks and begins to decline. Just as the news media becomes more brazenly ideological as it works to rescue and reconsolidate the ideological paradigm and framework it lives within; so with advertising, the question of whether the company/institution is even trying to market a product/service, or market ideology, comes to the fore. An advantage advertising has over something like news media however, is that advertising does not need to be bound by considerations of fact and objectivity - and if anything, is only bound by the requirements of profitability. This gives advertisers tremendous scope for what they deliver, and the freedom to align brand recognition and profit generation, with ideological content, narratives and scope.

In a sense this has always been true, and advertising has always exploited and utilized ideological trends or fashions (and trends of 'counter-culture') as a mechanic and tool. The difference really comes down to a question of degree; and the methodology that is employed in embedding and relaying ideological messaging. One thing that has certainly become more ubiquitous in the twilight years of the liberalist-globalist paradigm, is the exploitation of *emotionality* (or *hyper-emotionality*) as a marketing strategy. This is obvious with the advent of things like 'sadvertising', which is a form of micro-narrative building that is employed by advertisers and companies for the sake of having an extreme emotional effect on the viewer[70]. Excessive sentimentality and pathos are employed here, and many brands (such as major sports brands) like to exploit this as an effective marketing tool. It has become something of a cliché, that there is an emotional excess, or predominance, in our current, contemporary society and culture; and it is certainly true that a lot of what we find in media forms in general, is aimed at eliciting emotional responses[71].

The appeal to emotionality however, is more complex than just exploiting some readily available emotional template. Of course there are templates and universals that are easy to exploit and that people are susceptible to (if we think of how children are used as an emotional lynch-pin for instance). The *broader* operation and goal however, is in engineering the population to be receptive and moved by a *certain* emotional range and template *in*

---

[70] 'Sadvertising' really became more popular and ubiquitous with the advent of the millennium and in the 00's (although of course there were earlier precedents); and generally, the setting involves a kind of narrative that 'pulls at the heartstrings', and often won't even feature any product at all (but only the brand/entity that produced this mini-narrative).

[71] Sports channels rarely fail to mention emotion at some point during their broadcasting or advertising, and a kind of emotional fetishism has attached to sports consumption in general. Even the slow motion feature, that has become so normalized in televised sports broadcasting, is used to this end.

the first place. It is not sufficient that all and any emotional range be utilized or employed; but rather that a *certain* emotional structure and framework be established and utilized. This particular structure, is the one that enforces and drives ideological narratives; and more specifically, this emotional framework must be attached to a narrative structure, and find its significance and utilization within this structure. Once we begin to recognize the narrative framework and structure that emotionality is engineered for and within, then we begin to appreciate why emotional fetishism and focus, is so ubiquitous and central to advertising media (and, more broadly, any narrative based media).

The narrative system that forms the overall ideological input structure then, is enforced and reinforced through its attachment to a kind of hyper-emotionality. If you can engineer an individual, or group of individuals, to have an emotional response to *certain* content (a trigger) - regardless of whether this content be connected with reality/truth or not - then all you have to do is understand how to utilize this content (or trigger) to get the desired emotional reaction (and the narrative enforcement that comes with this). This is why the narrative-emotion relation works both ways, in an *inter-dependant relationship*; so that the narrative enforces the emotion, and the emotion enforces the narrative. Although this might lead to a chicken-and-egg question of which comes first (the narrative or the emotion), the truth is that both are engineered simultaneously, as part of the ideological construct within the broader ideological narrative. If we like, we can think of the narrative has having predominance, with the emotion being built around the narrative as reinforcement (where the narrative gains the energy and strength it needs to become a shaping one).

Advertising then, becomes a part of the input/output system we discussed in Chapter 3; where inputs ('code') are utilized for the sake of generating a reliable output. In this case, the input is the advertising data, that is designed to elicit an emotional response; and the output is the emotional response and the enforcing of the ideological narratives that this emotionality is designed to enforce. Being a part of the 'programming' system at large, is only to be expected from one of the most ubiquitous sectors in the world, whose job is to maximize profit and create brand omnipresence. Although emotionality and emotional manipulation is not the only technique used in advertising, it is certainly essential; not only because of its effectiveness as a marketing strategy, but because of its effectiveness as an *ideological strategy*. Again, the goal is not just to exploit an existing range of emotional tropes or devices; but to engineer the individual as a reliable system of outputs. If this can be engineered consistently and totally (through the cooperation of multiple industries and sectors), then a guaranteed product - a kind of machine - can be made. This is the individual as a *cipher*; and this individual, this unit, takes on the ideological body that it was engineered for (an apparatus of consistent outputs); whilst at the same time becoming a reliable consumer of content[72].

---

[72] Another way of thinking of the individual here, is the individual as a kind of *ideological effigy*. This is where the individual has become a living image of the system itself - its narratives, structures and 'values' - and has effectively become a *microcosm* of the ideological super-structure that surrounds them. This makes them *useful* as a *functional* replicate (effigy), in the sense that they too become drivers of ideological intent (functions of ideology). In becoming a body for the narratives that have shaped them; they live, reflect and enforce these narratives in the world they inhabit. In this way they become semi-autonomous and auto-functional, in the sense that they propagate these structures and narratives themselves, automatically. As an effigy, they are of course just a kind of copy (or replica); and lack the self-awareness of the ideological structure (and its over-engineers) that they are an image of. Insofar as this 'effigy' absorbs and receives inputs without much resistance, they are a safe metric for the system and its structures (a consistently reliable output); and can be largely trusted to consume and enforce narratives that have ideological function and impact. Financial profit is of course important in generating these units; but ideology is paramount: since the ideological effigy (that the consumer is), makes the whole thing operate in its present form; and inevitably creates demand for more content. Individuals desire this ideological content and messaging, since it has become central to the value and sustenance structures that the individual has just become an instance of: and their need for moral/ideological validation and reinforcement is delivered by having the right responses to the inputs. The consequences for the human psyche, and human society more generally, are profound and far-reaching: and if these media industries can refine and prolong their ideological and emotional grooming and targeting (as they have done); then they have developed an extremely powerful engineering tool (a kind of human weapon) for shaping and controlling human behavior almost totally.

Emotions and 'reality'

Without going too much into the philosophy of emotions, we should point out that an essential characteristic of emotions, is that they *do not need to map onto reality*. This is to say, that the emotional world and response set, can be totally enclosed within its own reality (that it then *projects* on to the outer world), whilst being totally detached from truth/objectivity (the actual outer world). In this sense the individual can be a totally contained ideological unit, that is moved and governed entirely by *unreality* (or their 'own reality'). It would be possible to conduct a set of experiments whereby individuals are engineered to have emotional responses (and beliefs connected to these emotions), that do not in any way reflect the objective world; but that only reflect a kind of artificial world (a false-reality). Such individuals would outwardly appear conventional and regular; but would actually be governed by inputs - and cognitive and non-cognitive patterns/structures[73] - that in no way reflect

---

[73] 'Non-cognitive' contrasts with 'cognitive'. 'Cognitive' (as we are using it, and as it is typically used), means data, or mental content, that is connected with conceptuality (to do with concepts and processing conceptual data). 'Non-cognitive', generally means mental or perceptive content that is non-conceptual. The taste of bread for instance, is a not a conceptual phenomenon, but something like a perception or sensation (that may be expressed in conceptual ways). Emotions are 'non-cognitive', in the sense that they are not primarily conceptual, but are a kind of sensation or 'feeling', that may or may not be, connected with conceptual (cognitive) data and information. It is not necessary to get hung-up

reality; but reflect an artificial construct (a false reality) that renders them *detached* from actual reality.

Constructing hypothetical's here is actually not even necessary, since the scenario described here is just the *actual* situation we face almost universally; especially since the advent of mass televised media. Of course, advertising and other media forms existed pre-televised media; but with the ubiquity and universality of televised (and then online) consumption, the entertainment and advertising industries gained tremendous reach. One of the most sure ways to maintain this reach and influence, is through emotional engineering; and creating realities for consumers that *need not bear upon the real world* (they rarely do), but that instead, bear upon the ideological construct itself.

Insofar as building these constructs requires a coordinated effort, it is no coincidence that all the major (and even minor) industries and sectors have unified messaging, 'values' and strategy. The increased need for ideological strategy and presence, prevents (at least for a while) any serious internal divisions within the system itself, and guarantees its effectiveness. This is why the narratives ultimately all align to deliver the same messages or super-narratives; and why the same patterns of emotional engineering are ubiquitous and universal. Universality of the message ultimately becomes the

---

on these definitions, and the sense of what these terms mean becomes clear through seeing how they are used in the text.

pattern, because again, absolute ideological homogenization is central to the liberalist-globalist project, and its structure as an ideological and political system. This means that all content, across all avenues, becomes increasingly controlled; with outliers and dissenters from mainstream narratives continually purged. This spirit of conformity and homogeneity actually just signals the death knell of these industries (at least their existing model); but because they are so trapped within their *own* unreality, they have no real ability to stem their increased irrelevance and rejection.

The television and movie industries

Before going any further, we should perhaps state that emotional content and messaging is not by itself inherently bad. One of the central premises of music, is that it is directed at us emotionally, and aims to move us via this emotional quality[74]. Again without going too much into the philosophy of emotions, we should recognize that emotions and reason (rationality) have a close relation; and that emotions should (in principle) hinge, and bear upon, rationality. This is to say that our emotions should be informed and governed by reason; so

---

[74] There is a lot more that could be said here vis-à-vis aesthetic theory, theories of music and their relation to emotions; but the point is that art productions have various standings in relation to our emotions - and music certainly stands in a strong direct relation to emotionality.

that, for instance, if some scenario, or incident was affecting us emotionally - but then we came to find that the information we were presented with was false or misleading - our emotions should accordingly adjust (i.e. we will generally no longer be moved by sympathy and empathy, when we find out that the individual we thought was the victim of an incident, was actually the perpetrator of that incident). In other words our emotions are (ideally) positioned to be corrected and shaped by the information we consume; and not the other way around. Misinforming people about a situation/narrative, so that you trigger certain emotional responses, is basic emotional manipulation.

With this being said, we can now move onto discussing the movie and television industries. The movie and television industries have had a tremendous effect on Western (and global) civilization since the earlier part of the 20th Century; and especially since the ubiquity of the television in practically every household in Western civilization (and then the world more generally). The movie industry has had a *total* influence (as opposed to just local or relative) on society, and, in unison with other media forms in general, has been one of the key engineers for mass societal shift. It has done this by being part of the universal coding system that programmes individuals and populations via narratives[75]. The

---

[75] 'Narratives' here can be taken to include: micro-narratives, general narratives, super-narratives, and symbolic content or messaging that enforces narratives.

ideological ambition of this industry and its players (those who drive and support its structures), only really became strongly evident, when the ideology it helped engineer peaked (and began to decline). Before that, this industry (like most industries), was mostly just taken at face value, as an 'entertainment industry'; and hardly considered an ideological mechanism at all. At best, it is thought of as an industry driven by power, wealth and celebrity (it of course is), and perhaps only in some very academic or esoteric circles, as being ideologically relevant.

The most significant way in which this industry reveals its ideological core and ambition, is through the content it injects into its productions. Again, the same patterns are present, and we observe that the ideological content and messaging is more blatant and brazen now, than previously. At one level this is a kind of self-affirmation, and indicator of ideological intent (and intolerance of dissent); and at another level it also reflects a form of panic and desperation, that threatens the core premise and structure of the industry. In accelerating ideological content and messaging though, it is not as though the industry has to do anything significantly new. No new methods are adopted; and only existing methods and tools are exploited, and used more forcefully. Of course, there are many methods and established techniques used to effectively tell a story and build a narrative (what the movie/film industry mostly does); but in terms of the most powerful *ideological* effect on the population; emotional engineering (the goal of building an ideologically emotional core and range for the viewer/public) is central.

We only need to fall back on what we have already stated about emotional engineering to understand why emotional states and responses are so carefully and intentionally engineered. It helps create an encased, self-sustaining, ideological value and belief set, that is set into motion via the input that is continuously given. It need have no actual connection with reality (non-fiction), but becomes its own powerful arbiter and force of momentum. The movie industry as a engineer of fiction narratives, is especially apt for this purpose; even where the fiction is disguised or presented as non-fiction. On the face of it, it is actually quite remarkable that fictional narratives, and someone playing a fictional role (or a fictional role disguised as non-fiction), has had such a tremendous effect on our collective psyche - and this is something to do with the art form inherent to narrative construction. The narrative has to *move* its audience, and it elicits and draws an emotional response from its audience *by design*. This is the power inherent to this discipline, and a large part of the reason a certain actor, or actress, will be revered (through the conviction with which they play their *role*, and art with which they get the viewer to sympathize/associate/empathize with the character they play[76]).

---

[76] Or whatever other set of emotional responses the viewer is supposed to get from the characters role. This may be negative (a

So even on the face of it, we concede that film/movie production and story building, is largely directed at eliciting emotional responses from the audience. This is certainly nothing new, and is as old as the discipline of story-telling itself. What is characteristic of the industry in its current form though, is the ideological goal the narrative building is directed toward. One of the main tools here, that is pretty well established by now, is the device of the *victim narrative*[77]. This is a structure where production companies manufacture and finance narratives (and this messaging can be explicit or more subtle), whereby certain groups, or individuals, are presented and portrayed as a victims. We could, again, go into the psychology and philosophy of victim politics, and why the politics of victimhood is so powerful and ubiquitous (it is certainly extremely common to see it in the political sphere, and, as we already discussed, within news media narratives); but the central premise and rationale is straightforward enough. If you can make the

---

villain for instance), positive (a victim or hero for instance) or ambivalent, etc.

[77] At this point it may be suspected that I am diminishing, or failing to recognize, the significance of what it really means to be a victim; or something along those lines. I do not, not comprehend the import and significance of what it means to be a real victim of something. What I am talking about here though, is the *mask* of victimhood; or where victimhood is *weaponized* for political and ideological gain. This is an extremely powerful, very common, form of social engineering (where there is reluctance to challenge the narratives as they are presented - mostly due to fear and optics). Actual victims rarely get the attention and justice they deserve – especially if they are victims of the ideological structures themselves.

audience feel 1: sympathy, and/or 2: guilt, with regard to a situation/occurrence; then you can control all (or most of) the surrounding emotional and cognitive responses that situation/occurrence is built into. This is very important, and part of the reason fictionality has a power that exceeds the sphere of fiction itself[78].

With victim narratives then, the target is very much the audience, their emotions and their belief (or 'value') set. The slogan 'the personal is political', is used to express the idea that even the personal and private spheres of human life have political significance: but we could equally say 'the victim is political'; since one of the most characteristic features of our late capitalist, liberalist-globalist paradigm, is the politics of *victimhood*, and the targeting of the population with victim narrative constructs. What is most characteristic of the film/fiction/narrative industry at large though, is how narratives of victimhood are generally detached from actuality; and exist largely within their own closed realm of fiction and ideological construction. This is of course the point, and the art here is to present the

---

[78] Guilt, like trauma, is an extremely powerful operative in the human psyche, and can have a wide reaching influence on human behaviors. Guilt itself (especially when used as psychological tool) is typically a form of trauma. It operates as a kind of unconscious monitor over both the cognitive build (what the individual thinks, believes, etc), and the non-cognitive build (emotions, feelings); and can thereby regulate, control and limit individual behavior. If a whole population segment can be made to harbor guilt, then that segment is open to mass paralysis, manipulation and control.

story/scenario *as though* it were just a mirror of reality and objectivity; when it is in fact a mirror of its own ideological intent and structure (that is passed off *as though* it were reality). When victim narratives are built effectively (as they often are), they are another extremely powerful engineering tool; not least of all because the consumer of the content has little-to-no idea they are being manipulated with a fabricated 'reality'.

If the consumer does ever begin to suspect that he is being engineered for ideological reasons (and that they are not just watching 'entertainment' or consuming 'art'); then their resentment and hostility toward this industry in its extent form (and perhaps as such), is likely to grow. If this awareness increases more universally, then we can expect a swift demise of both the cult of celebrity, and the uncritical uptake of ideological narratives. This is largely what we are currently witnessing with regard to the movie/film industry; although we cannot say that the population at large are aware, or are even interested, in these ideological strategies (and there is a significant segment of the population that support and enforce these narratives in any case). If there was a good reason why skepticism and resentment toward the narrative-construction-industries continues to grow (along with their corresponding loss of power and influence), it is because of ideological content being sold under the guise of something else (very much in the same way that the mainstream 'news' media sells its content under the guise of something else). The entertainment industry is supposed to be about entertainment (at least this is a popular notion); and movies are supposed to entertain, or (in certain cases), be representatives of an art form. As such, they cannot brazenly be *functions of ideology* and political tools: lest they sacrifice both the 'entertainment' role, and the 'art' role, and locate themselves firmly within the political and ideological sphere (as they have done). Sacrificing the principle rationale of your disciple/profession for ideological purposes and a political agenda, whilst wearing the mask of something else, is basic subversion[79].

Narratives and division strategy

It is of course, not to be expected that everything should be in perfect keeping with its main function and ostensible purpose. There is a good argument for the idea that ideology is always present to some degree, in any cultural manifestation; and we do not expect total ideological purity. Moreover, we expect that art and narratives will deal with political and ideological subjects,

---

[79] The question of whether something can function as propaganda (ideological content), and still retain an art function (or be considered 'art'), is subject to philosophical debate. The subject ties in with the idea of whether art must be 'disinterested' and in what way. Suffice to say that if an individual discovered that a movie, book, narrative, or piece of music that they loved - subtly embedded political or ideological messaging they opposed, or just found to be false - it would come as no surprise that they lose their love for this narrative or work (at least to a degree).

as they always have done, since these subjects are highly topical and built into the fabric of daily living. But there is a difference between inherent ideological structure within any cultural paradigm and epoch, and overt and subversive ideological engineering for precisely defined ideological and political objectives (many of which are unprecedented in human history). A digital entertainment and film industry with universal reach, is a relatively new phenomenon; and coincides with the rise of capitalistic, neo-liberalist globalism, in general. It is only inevitable that as soon as this industry begins to experience serious resistance and a lack of steady incremental increase in popularity, consumption and ideological influence; that it will ramp up its ideological operations significantly. As a major functionary of the system and its ideological structure, it really *has* to mobilize in this way, and unreflectively does so. As a result, it naturally employs the same strategies that the system at large uses; so that exploiting *division politics* and *division strategy* - even more than it already has - also becomes central here.

In the case of the mainstream media, we seen that division engineering is part of the overall strategy for maintaining and reconsolidating ideological power (a 'divide-and-conquer' strategy). We discussed how engineering demographic division and warfare is essential to this end, and that by weaponizing the politics of 'identity' (racial divisions, sex divisions, etc), they are able to divide the populations along tribalistic and demographic lines; complete with a population of 'victims' and a population of non-victims (or the 'guilty'). They do this largely though building narratives that carry the appearance of being 'news', even though for the most part, they are just carefully selected pieces of 'information' that usually exclude, either the context they are embedded within, or just the broader picture in general. Ultimately, the same narrative building techniques are used in the case of film fiction or entertainment; with the difference that the 'news' media, have to embed and construct their narratives, totally under the pretence and disguise of them being *non-fiction*.

Film is different and interesting, because the narratives it presents are ostensibly fiction (or largely fiction[80]), but where the internal component is ultimately, grounded in reality. By this we mean the internal psychological and emotional world of the characters and their interactions, is supposed to mirror, or bear upon, the real world. Story building is, in most cases, the construction of a narrative *as though* it were reality (or an image of reality); and this is what their effectiveness and power consists in. To this end, the production must move, or affect the viewer in some way that relates to the actual human world: and this is to say that our engagement with narratives, has to, in some essential way, connect with our cognitive and

---

[80] Even stories that are based on 'real life' occurrences, are fictitious in construct, and typically use an actual world occurrence as a kind of gateway.

emotional range, and their basis in the world of actual human relations and interactions[81]. Without this component, there would be no meaningful narrative at all; and no anchor for the story to be effective within.

Despite this need to be anchored in 'reality' however, a kind of blurring occurs; and the distinction between fiction and non-fiction (or reality) breaks down: insofar as 'reality' begins to operate under the influence (of a 'new reality') created by the fiction constructs themselves[82]. When the world of fiction (or art) begins to shape individual value, belief and judgment norms (or their 'ideal' norms); then that is an input system (in this case narratives) having real world outputs. This *new reality*, that is built by the narrative constructs (and the super-narratives that surround us), becomes for the individual, the 'real world' that they live in. This is how powerful narratives and super-narratives are, and why they are engineered so carefully and continuously - since they

---

[81] Of course there are stories that do not function like conventional narratives, but might be heavily surrealist or symbolic, for instance. Even in these cases, the symbolic import and significance is grounded in the actual human condition.

[82] The idea I am expressing here is not new or novel, but is related to the concept of 'hyperreality' - as that term was used in certain post-modern philosophies; most notably that of Jean Baudrillard (1929-2007). The concept of hyperreality is much broader and complex than we have discussed here; although we have expressed a basic component of it in certain respects. As a philosophical concept, it developed with the advent and growth of our technological, media saturated age; although it would take us too much out of the way, to discuss the concept any more than is needed for our purposes here.

become and enforce the ideological 'reality' that the individual (and group/population) now inhabit, and that reflects itself in their collective behaviors. And this is just the overall goal of ideological messaging and engineering; so that the narrative content that is input and shapes the individual into a certain form (a kind of living effigy), is effective across a broad population range progressively over time.

Understanding the ideological role of 'entertainment' media then, enables us to appreciate why the narratives employed, are so victim politics focused; and why this category is so crucial[83]. Once you have successfully built narratives of oppression and victimhood for certain groups and demographic segments; then whoever controls these narratives and the triggers built into them, just becomes a kind of social engineer (or director). Apart from the experience of power this role gives them; these engineers know how to set into motion and utilize the energy, momentum and *political power* that the narrative

---

[83] I recognize that a post-modern perspective might want to maintain the open-narrative potential of any narrative produced (where different people take away 'different things' from what they saw/read; and there is no 'fixed', or master narrative, etc). This might be an interesting philosophical approach, but the actual production, as it is delivered to the consumer, is systematically and overwhelmingly engineered to produce ideological narratives that affect the audience in an ideological (and political) way. We should also remember that in many respects, post-modernism was a total failure as a philosophy for living; insofar as the open-narrative and multiple-possibility world it appeared to advocate for, was neglected in favor of ideological and narrative absolutism.

construct has created (which for the individuals or groups in question, is never a false construct, but their actual reality)[84]. These social engineers ultimately find their greatest strength and effectiveness, in a unified structure (a kind of club); where this unity guarantees precision and coordinated effectiveness.

The public (or audience)that these social engineers target however, is not unified: and there must be a concerted effort to maintain divisions within the populations at large - as long as the ideological project is not totally consolidated and cemented (and even beyond that). The 'victim' segment of the population (individuals whose identity is shaped by victim narratives), must necessarily co-exist with a perpetrator (the guilty) segment, and be counter-balanced by it. Once these narratives are fully operational and effective, you then have *two* effective functions for the ideological structure at large. First the 'victims'; that will largely, and by design, be monopolized

---

[84] We needn't think of these narratives as being obvious political or ideological narratives, with an overt victim or political narrative blatantly on the surface. This sometimes does happen, but it is more often that these narratives, or themes, are embedded much more subtly; so that for instance, the viewer is lead to sympathize with this person because of some injustice, or led to see the humanity in this person, where it was not expected, or led to dislike some character because of some portrayed negative that affected another, etc, etc. Contemporary narratives are saturated with these small things, that effect the viewer emotionally and cognitively. Again, the blurring between fiction and non-fiction, and extent to which these narratives begin to shape and function *as* reality; is significant - and just part of the overall ideological design.

by 'minority groups'; and who will be moved easily in the relevant ideological direction, simply by pulling the right strings (typically using 'freedom', 'equality', 'empowerment' and 'oppression' narratives): and secondly, the 'perpetrator' segment, who through the paralysis and shame of the guilt (trauma) system, will be exceedingly eager to *redeem themselves* (morally and socially speaking), by whatever is signaled or promoted as a being morally redeeming. This need for moral redemption and affirmation can be so strong, that it creates generations of activists[85], whose motivation is to make sure other 'perpetrators' (guilty ones) suffer the same sense of humiliation and low sense of self-worth they themselves feel. In becoming ideologically and politically active, even against their own interests and well being, they seek redemption and validation through becoming useful functionaries (or proxies) for the ideological system at large[86].

Other industries and sectors

So all industries, sectors, institutions and agencies of liberalist-globalist ideology and objectives, are invested in

---

[85] By 'activists' we just mean individuals who are ideologically active; but it could mean activists as they are part of an institutionalized or organized activism.

[86] This partly explains the phenomenon of 'virtue signaling', which is the need or express moral opinion or value, through (artificially) signaling certain moral values or principles (or at least what is being sold (signaled) as a moral value or principle).

delivering the same narratives, super narratives and messaging: and this is clear enough in how controlled and censorious these structures become, and in their own ideological homogenization. The advertising sectors are as invested in identity politics and constructing victim identities (and thereby 'guilt' identities), just as much as the 'entertainment' industries and the 'news' media are. It is also not just delivering particular narratives, but cultivating an *overall individual type*, that must be highly susceptible to emotional and non-cognitive influences; that then contribute to the cognitive make-up and psychological world these individuals inhabit. This is the ideological cipher (or effigy) that we spoke of; and a weighted emotionality that is detached from the prerogative and weight of rationality, is fundamental in driving narratives that are effective to the point of near total control. The super-narratives have to saturate all spheres of human life; and to this end, the media structures must be totally ubiquitous and omnipresent. Globalism in its later stages, in many ways, just becomes this form of narrative omnipresence and absolutism; and media saturation is useful to this end.

Before moving onto Chapter 5 (and *Part 2* of this book) it is worth mentioning some of the other media industries/sectors that we might have already mentioned in passing. Again, many of the same patterns and methodologies persist; and this is only to be expected from a coordinated and unified ideological structure and system, that has a common and exact set of goals.

The music industry

The music industry is obviously a massive industry (or set of industries) that has been imported globally[87]. It is no secret that music is emotionally directed and can have a strong emotional impact; and music's ability to move people and induce certain emotional states - from extreme sadness to extreme elevation - is one of the main reasons it is employed in advertising and the entertainment/movie industry in general. It is naturally wedded to narrative production, because narrative production aims at eliciting emotional states and responses. Music can, by itself though, create its own narratives, particularly when joined with lyrics: and these narratives are further re-enforced when the music piece is accompanied with a music video; that enforces the narrative either explicitly or symbolically. The contemporary music industry is characteristically narrative based, and narratives saturate the whole musical structure and its delivery.

Apart from our earlier points about the implicit and inherent ideology of all cultural productions within any given era period (and this will be certainly true of music), we need not say that every song, or piece of music, is directed toward overt political or ideological messaging. In the later stages (and decline) of the ideological

---

[87] Music itself is obviously as old as civilization, but I am referring here to the (popular) music *industry*, as the product of a liberal, capitalist, Western civilization.

paradigm however, ideological messaging and intent increases drastically; and the exact same strategy and intent we discussed with regard to the 'news' media and 'entertainment' industries, is at work in the music production. The extra advantage here though, is that the medium (the media) is largely emotive, so that unlike the news media that has to dress its narratives under the guise of 'news' and factuality (non-fiction); music lacks this restriction in its ideological construct. Of course, it is not totally without front, and what the music industry mostly wants to dress itself as, is *art*. Hence the title of 'artist' for any piece of music that is released; and this, at the least, lends the impression that overt ideological messaging and engineering is not in the foreground.

The lyrical content then, is useful and important to the music construct when this is functioning ideologically. At some level, the tempo, or rhythm, must resonate with the listener, and this tempo can convey an extremely broad emotional range itself[88]. The scope of lyrical content is unlimited to whatever message or narrative

---

[88] If we think of rap music for instance; rap as it has been imported from street culture (where it had its original meaning), into pop music, is really about energizing or empowering the individual with certain concepts and ideas, that are placed within a kind of repetitive, rhythmic lyrical tempo. The lyrics in this rap-pop setting are mostly throw-away and gimmicky; and are really designed for a kind of hyper-empowerment of the audience (that the audience enjoys and then craves). But these lyrics can also have an ideological role and function; and serve to empower and energize the individual as an ideological unit, that has become addicted to being energized in this way.

the lyricist wants to convey; and therefore the ideological scope is also very broad. It is of course, not always the case that the music piece is overtly ideological; and an analysis of narrative categories would probably show that the love ballad (a variation on this theme), is the most ubiquitous and universal form of music narrative. Even here though, there is large scope for ideological engineering; and even just a passing remark can be part of a larger ideological narrative structure.

By way of example, we might look at how the concept of 'freedom' functions in musical lyrics; and particularly 'freedom' as a regular motif in 1990's pop and dance music. At one level, this term is just a useful device for injecting content and giving some kind of meaning to the music: but at another level, the function here is a kind of ideological reinforcement through the repetition and placement of the term (in the narrative construct). The term 'freedom' as it is and was used, mostly functions in harmony with already pre-existing ideas of freedom. These ideas of freedom are typically very surface, in that they are primarily aligned with a heavily individualistic and hedonistic framework: and it is no surprise that the concept aligns with liberalist populist values or ideology in general. It is also superficial and empty in the sense that these concepts of 'freedom', exist in a system and societal structure of relative *unfreedom*. We might also be suspicious about the meaningful use of the term in a pop-musical setting, where the force of emotion dominates and supersedes the rational, or analytical, use of a concept or idea. It would be foolish to expect philosophical precision and conceptual coherence from song lyrics in pop music of course; but it is not as though the concepts and their placement are not ideological[89]. A great deal of ideological significance is carried just in the seemingly casual use of a concept (or narrative), and its placement within an emotional setting (input): and the combination here of tempo and concepts (in the lyrics) is extremely influential and formative; especially given the younger audience that a lot of music targets. Understanding how to combine concepts with feelings of euphoria (or sentimentality, or other emotional ranges), is understanding how the music production is able to inject ideological messaging and narratives; without having to deliver coherent conceptual information that can be scrutinized as being 'false'. Music is rarely, if ever, evaluated for its coherence with conceptuality and factuality, since that is supposed to be largely irrelevant to the power and meaning of music in the first place.

It is fair to say that the same threats that face the film and movie industries (which we discussed), now face the contemporary music industry (or industries) as well (since they are all part of the same ideological super-structure).

---

[89] It is in principle possible that music convey true (or real) meaning through its content; and this does happen (and meaning can of course be given just through the non-lyrical music construct itself). However, the typical placement of terms and narratives - and even the non-lyrical music construct itself - is often in service of ideological narratives and structures.

Musicians that were once idolized and heavily revered, just no longer have the same influencing and cultural power, in that they are no longer taken seriously as a voice for moral normativity or social change (except within a relatively closed echo chamber)[90]. The only celebrity opinions that have a kind of reverberance and force now, are those that are actually likely to upset the liberalist-globalist narratives that are typically conveyed (although this is risky, potentially career ending and rarely happens). The plethora of musical productions, and the music industry itself, is subject to increased cynicism with regard to its ideological over-reach and intent[91]; and

---

[90] The music industry as we currently know it, was driven (in the 50's, 60's and 70's) by a so-called 'counter-culture'. This 'counter-culture' rebelled against inheritance and established norms (hence it being 'counter') in favor of a new expression (artistic and cultural) and ideology (and we discussed these issues in Chapter 2). Now that this 'counter-culture' has largely achieved its objectives, and helped bring about our liberalist-globalist paradigm, it is no longer 'counter'; since it is now just the cultural and social norm. This was never really a movement of 'rebellion' to begin with, but a movement into a radically increased form of social and ideological control (even though many of the players did not really understand what they were actually standing for and inducing). Because the 'counter-culture' no longer stands for anything 'counter', but has just become the culture in general, its advocates stand in an inverse position to what they used to, and actually have a counter-culture up against them.

[91] The tools of ideological reach and control are not just straightforwardly limited to 'emotions'. For instance, the hyper-sexualization and obnoxiousness of the music industry (especially when joined with music video), and motifs and gestures of attitude and 'nonconformity'; all form part of the content and strategy for gaining market and ideological relevance and position generally

this cynicism is certainly warranted because the productions are increasingly hyper-ideological in function[92]. The omnipresence and availability of popular music, along with its refinement as a medium that can influence the viewer emotionally, guarantees that such a medium will be useful for ideological messaging and content, for as long as this particular model survives[93].

Magazine formats

An underrated candidate for ideological influence perhaps, but certainly a key sector, and with a large consumer base. Needless to say, there is an extremely broad range of interests covered by the magazine industry at large, even if the ideological range is limited by the structure of this industry (in terms of what will be allowed to be a part of the distribution and publication networks). This limit is evident enough in the political

---

(although these things will *connect* with emotions in important ways).

[92] We should also remember the ideological impact and power of the music video, that is often consumed with the music itself.

[93] The notion that music will 'unite people', is palpably false. At best, music as a local/regional/national phenomenon and expression; is a feature of an *already* unified people (for instance in more closed historical communities and nations). It is a romantic (and false) idea in the extreme, that music by itself, has unifying power within an ideologically divided nation, or group. At best it brings together people who are already more or less in ideological affinity (or have a common interest). Music is not the kind of thing that can transcend and reunite true ideological division; even if it does allow some groups or individuals to share a common interest.

domain for instance; where, even though there is a range of different magazines, the ideological range is certainly narrow. Readily available political (or 'current affairs') magazines, are mostly just an extension and manifestation of the corporate mainstream media structures and ownership; and their range and content is just a continuation and reflection of the 'legacy', or mainstream media, platforms. Political magazines usually come with the added veneer of intellectuality however, and a kind of conservatism of format is maintained in the magazine format and delivery; even if conservatism is, by and large, rejected by this industry. Because their audience is more ostensibly 'high brow'; they are more effectively able to dress their ideological intent and messaging under this guise of conceptual depth. There are of course, some instances of good, analytical and more objective content (articles); although for the most part, these magazines are another cog in the engine of narrative engineering (which is to say, they are also functions of ideology).

It depends on the location, but generally, political magazines do not make up the bulk of readily available purchase point magazines: and it just takes a casual glance at the magazine range in a local store or supermarket/hypermarket, to recognize that a significant segment of the consumer audience is female - with a high volume of 'lifestyle' magazines and 'entertainment' (or 'gossip') magazines. 'Gossip', or 'entertainment' magazines, thrive on *drama*; with drama being very much the core appeal. It is probably a inherent part of human nature to enjoy and fetishize drama, but the consumption of drama and its forms are certainly not ideological neutral. A culture with a high media drama content, tends to seek those forms of drama - and whatever drama tropes or types exist, will be mirrored in the lives of its consumers. It is not uncommon for people to engineer and foment a kind of soft-drama in their own lives, because of the drama they consume and enjoy. This is a kind of *emotional* drama; and this soft-drama that the individual(s) build around themselves, becomes heavily fetishized and indulged. At some level, it is almost as though the consumer of drama, and those that have taken up pop-drama fetishism, are only capable of finding worth, energy and meaning in their lives, through these soft-drama constructs[94]. These constructs mirror the 'entertainment' constructs that saturate the magazine content (and larger sections of the entertainment industry), and thus become a part of the false reality (or hyperreality) that becomes its own self-contained structure. These dramas are not ideologically neutral, because they typically embed ideological content: and it is not difficult to imagine forms of fetishistic drama that

---

[94] We say 'soft-drama', because hard-drama is exhausting and traumatizing to the point of anxious tension and exhaustion (that is difficult to sustain over the long run). However, even the hard-drama can, for certain individuals and in certain cases, be a point of fetishistic enjoyment - where a lot of attention and drama is pulled towards the individual and the drama they inhabit (especially if they mirror dramas that circulate culturally).

center around narratives of victimhood, or 'bigotry', or 'discrimination'; and that actually develop a capacity for real world influence (i.e. for shaping and creating policies). This is why drama, the fetishism of drama, and the drama narrative construct, are very effective as ideological tools; and intentionally cultivated into magazine, entertainment and other media structures. In most cases, the driving momentum of drama is emotional, and a set of emotional reactions based upon a fetishistic hyperreality (or unreality); and 'reality television' is very much an extension of these drama narrative constructs.

'Lifestyle' magazines aimed at both females and males (although largely females), also tend to operate under the pretence of being 'educational' and 'informative'. If we think of the parent-child relationship by way of analogy to a nation and its citizens (not a precise analogy, but with significance), then globalism is not only the attempt to strip the nation of absolute power (and transfer, and reconsolidate that power into trans-national government, institutions, sectors, agencies, etc) - it is also the ambition to strip power away from the parent (parental authority and rights), and transfer that power to extra-parental entities, such as the educational, local-governmental and other state controlled institutions (that are themselves under the authority of supranational entities and institutional set-ups and dictates). This transfer of power to the extra-parental, and away from the parent, must be prepared and introduced gradually; so that the child willingly sides with the extra-parental structures (what the child has effectively been groomed for), and the parent willingly give up the role of parent to the extra-parental (and receive a kind of diminished responsibility as a reward[95]). The 'educational' content embedded in magazines (and other sectors), is typically just another supplanting of the role of the parent, and a *wedge* driven between the child and parental influence and authority[96]. Insofar as parental roles and structures have already

---

[95] Although a significant amount of *legal* responsibility and liability will remain with the parent.

[96] 'Sex' (as in sexual intercourse and everything that surrounds it) forms a lot of the content of lifestyle magazines aimed at younger people; and these magazines, like entertainment media in general, have successfully pushed the boundaries to target increasingly younger audiences with sex related content. The sexualization of children is a real phenomenon, and this sexualization is largely by design. But to what end? Rather than go into this at depth (although it would be interesting to do so), suffice to say that the purpose of this sexualization (that may or may not be under the guise of 'education' and teaching 'responsible behavior'), is to create *sexual promiscuity*. Engineering promiscuity is (ironically) a kind of neutering device; whereby the possibility of functional long term relations, and the creation of a successful 'nuclear family', is significantly jeopardized and damaged. Young females are largely targeted for this purpose (although males as well), and of course we recognize narratives of 'freedom' and 'liberation' are connected with this objective. Individuals unable to function within long term family and marriage relations, are far more likely to turn to the state and globalist structures, as a kind of surrogate and security; and will overwhelmingly support and validate these super-structures, and the narratives of validation that they provide. This is particularly true when single-parenthood is involved (typically single mothers), and a useful device for the liberalist-globalist system, is broken families (hence their proliferation).

been cultivated into ineffectiveness and volatility, then in most cases, this is a fairly easy task to achieve.

The environment

It would be possible to make a case for the environment itself, as a form of 'media'; but it would somewhat abstract and obtuse. What is important here is to understand how the environment is *used* as a huge resource for media placement, control and exploitation. Of course the term 'environment' is itself vague, and tends to suggest either the 'natural' environment (nature), or just the area that surrounds and contains life (plant, animal, human). It is no secret that the 'urban environment' is heavily laden and saturated with various forms a media, especially advertising media - but it is also true that even more rural environments are not lacking in media placement. In many ways, a lot of media content is now what we might call trans-locational, insofar as we have a perpetual array of media delivered via television and internet sources, along with a huge increase in portability (portable devices). Nevertheless, environmentally situated media still plays an extremely significant role within the input/output system, and there are some important sociological -or philosophical - points to be observed.

First, is that we recognize that our environment, for a large part, is a system of symbols, or signs. Thus things we might normally take for granted, such as road signs and road markings for instance; actually play a broader symbolic role beyond their surface, or ostensible, function. There was a point where country, or rural roads (which were relatively free from excessive markings and indicators), became more littered with signs and signage. The rationale behind this is usually something like increased road safety; but there is actually a subtle ideological function behind this increase of signs and control systems. Likewise, if we think of contemporary vehicles, the range of computerized symbols, messaging and function indicators, is significantly increased, and continues to increase. The rationale is again, increased ease and safety; but there is actually an excess and coercion, that mirrors and symbolizes the increased control, coercion and regulation in day to day life as such (and that inevitably comes with top-down, global regulatory control systems). The relentless increase and chase of state and institution induced regulations and controls, reflects itself in the sign structure that surrounds us; and this is not accidental, but follows as a matter of cause-and-effect. It is a kind of imprint of the macrocosm (the over-structure) in the microcosm (the smaller-structures), and the end result is a symbolic *reification* in the environment that surrounds us, that replicates and symbolizes the consolidated, institutionalized, globalist ideological schema, at large.

Building structures and architectural styles are also an instance of this. Where the architectural style of a period might be said to reflect the norms, ideals, philosophy and spirit of the age they are built within; it is not insignificant that in our current epoch, we found the move toward a non-diverse, pared-down building style - reduced to pure homogenized functionality and economic minimalism[97]. This minimalism requires that the building be able to stand within a certain regulatory framework and is cheap to build; and this is certainly the rationale behind contemporary mass building projects (housing estates/units, apartment blocks, industrial units, etc). The logic of neo-liberalist globalism will inevitably reflect its character at the production and material level; and aesthetic brutalism, extreme standardization, continuous rapid expansion and homogenization, are just inherent to this (and ironically (or perhaps not) it comes very close in spirit to what socialism delivers). Again, we shouldn't think of these things as accidental, but as an extension of the ideology as such. And because this ideology is very anxious to bring all individuals under its remit and authority, we can expect that its expansion and reach - even at the level of signage and 'style' - to be expansive and absolute. This means the whole environment - urban, suburban and rural - are targets for symbolic reification.

---

[97] There is a popular notion that we have moved towards increased 'diversity'; and that this is an inherent good. This is actually false; and the liberalist-globalist paradigm at its end point, seeks only 'diversity' at a superficial level, and aims to annihilate *actual diversity*, in favor of the total homogeneity of belief, speech, 'values' and acceptable ideology. A homogenized populace and world, is far easier to control and engineer, for both economic and social purposes.

These environmental symbols, signs and structures, are 'inputs' just as much as direct ideological messaging is, and make the individual more receptive (or normalized) to the overall ideology as such[98].

Apart from this more symbolic and abstract level of inputs however, there are the more regular media inputs that are fairly standard in the environment more generally (particularly our urban environments). This media is largely in the form of static brand advertising: although we also find televised content and televised 'news' media around us often enough. Many of the brands we encounter are owned by the same entities that own the mainstream news media; and this is especially true of 'entertainment' brands, and brands targeting children. The centralization of ownership is very useful of course, insofar as it enables ideological homogenization across multiple media avenues; and allows a more precise and controlled ideological engineering and narrative building[99]. Because of this ideological pay-off, urban environments are highly crafted and engineered (ideologically speaking); so that

---

[98] We can apply this equally to our indoor, or interior environments, which are also symbolically and structurally significant.

[99] It is no accident that the corporate world is in total ideological unity and affinity with all other institutions and industries. By this we mean that the corporate world (including 'big tech') shares the exact same ideological framework and intent as the: entertainment industries, news media industries, arts sectors/industries, educational institutions, multiple NGO/'Human Rights' organizations and globalist institutions, banks, 'think tanks' and industries more generally.

even if the profit generated by advertising were marginal (and it is never possible to calculate actual profit from broad advertising), advertising would still be desired and present - simply because it is an extremely effective way to embed ideological content and messaging. Urban locales, in many ways, carry the highest stakes; since they are largely the stronghold and bastion for the liberalist-globalist paradigm in *real terms*. This is just to say that when it comes to voting and voter turnout; by far the largest turnout for the established liberalist-globalist paradigm and its representation at the political level, is amongst the populations that inhabit urban environments (i.e. cities and large towns)[100]. If we were to display ideological affiliation on a global map, then the hubs and major centers of those that seek liberalist-globalist policy and establishments, would be located in urban environments. The presence of high media saturation is not accidental to this phenomenon, and there will be no neglect of the urban environment as a key *ideological node*[101].

---

[100] A casual glance at voting patterns will testify to this; and accounts for the reason why a presidential candidate in the U.S. can still lose the Presidential Election, whilst nevertheless having won the 'popular vote'.

[101] In terms of image saturation, both the high street and shopping malls are extremely high saturation, mostly in the form of brand advertising via the fashion industry. The fashion industry itself is an extremely ideological industry, although we will not be discussing this as a separate category here. Suffice to say that they exploit the same narrative building techniques other industries, or sectors exploit. Generations of children brought up in shopping malls is

Summary

There is a lot more we could discuss in this chapter, and there are media sectors and industries that we have not even touched upon (such as social media and the 'arts' industries more generally)[102]. Focusing on the ideological reach and intent of all media forms, would be a project of at least book length: and for our purposes here, we have discussed many of the most important factors. *Narrative building* has been perhaps our main focus in this chapter, since in many respects, this is the heart and most essential function of entertainment and advertising industries when they are functioning ideologically. *Super-narratives* dictate the direction and content of all smaller narratives or pieces of data - whether that be a TV show, 'news' segment or even just a single image used in advertising - and one of the key super-narratives, is the super-narrative of *victimhood*. Victim politics is absolutely essential to an already peaked, liberalist-globalist

---

almost a guarantee of strong ideological influence, and will help super-engineer the ideological individual and consumer that the system depends upon. The questions of why and how this works are complex, although we have touched upon a number of these factors.
[102] We have also not discussed things like search engines; and online encyclopedias and dictionaries. Online 'encyclopedias' are important, because they make a very strong pretence of information impartiality and objectivity; when in fact they are extremely ideological in how they present and control information. We also have not discussed things like 'dating-apps' and the mass prevalence and saturation of pornography. Pornography (especially extreme pornography) is also interesting, because the population in general have no idea how significant this is in ideological engineering, and in many ways is a key mechanic in the liberalist-globalist ideological structure and design.

paradigm, and its ambition for a total re-consolidation of power and control. Narratives of victimhood, inevitably come with guilt narratives; and so division strategy is an essential part of the game here. These engineered super-narratives are not an abstraction, since they have actually become 'reality' for the individual or group (a hyperreality), that function *as though* they were an objective reality. These constructs have to be absolutely real to the individual, since their 'reality' is the energy that drives the individual as an ideological unit, cipher or effigy. If they ceased to be 'real' it would diminish and cripple the ideological energy and movement that comes with victim constructs: and there is no other reality outside of this ideologically engineered one[103]. If someone were to threaten these narratives - not only would they face a violent reaction - they would face a kind of excommunication from any environment where those narratives dominate. In the current climate these narratives exist everywhere, and form a large part of the energetic basis of the activism and politics of this ideology. It is why these participants benefit from high media saturation to begin with; since this saturation and narrative omnipresence is a constant reinforcing of the ideological super-narratives[104]. It also means that older

---

[103] This is concisely summarized in a phrase by Nietzsche: 'Understanding kills action, action depends on a veil of illusion'. (BT 7:39). See bibliography for details.

[104] There are more super-narratives than just victimhood. An idea of societal 'progress' (progressivism) is another super-narrative, and there are many others. As a matter of economy, it would be possible

forms of media content (older movies for instance), that existed prior to a more refined cultivation of ideological narratives, could be outright purged from memory and circulation[105]. Fundamentally, any individuals who do not accept (or reject) the super-narratives; becomes an enemy of both the 'system', and the individuals who support this system (those whose cognitive and non-cognitive apparatus is built by the system via inputs): and the conditions for radical ideological division are in place from this alone. What we head toward - in terms of broader ideological warfare - is a polarization of individuals who are *for* (are a part of) the ideological system, and those who are *against* the ideological system, its narratives and its super-structures[106].

---

to build a hierarchy of narratives and super-narratives, and perhaps even something above the super-narrative, or something that contains even those.

[105] This is true of many areas however, including history and other forms of literature; and why 'humanities', or academic disciplines more broadly, are just as susceptible to being ideological functionaries (they in many ways are).

[106] Interestingly, many individuals who at this point claim to be 'against the system', are actual agents or tools of the system. They just don't recognize the extent to which they are tools, or proxies, of globalist control and engineering. It is easy to tell who these individuals and groups are, because the broader system in general (that they typically defend), is in support of them, and builds a kind of firewall around them and their narratives (narratives that have been given to them by the system and its structures in the first place).

Conclusion to *Part 1*

This is the end of *Part 1* of this book, and *Part 2* will follow in due course. What I hope the reader takes from this first part, is the extent to which a lot of the information and structures around us, that we generally take for granted, are actually *functions of ideology* (or means of ideological engineering). Once we recognize this, we are then in a position to, 1: understand better the character and reality of our political situation; and 2: understand why society is divided in the way that it is. In understanding point 2 better, we also recognize that societal division is not totally fortuitous, or *just* something that develops with differences amongst populations; but is *actively engineered* for the purposes of political and ideological control. After all is said and done, the strategy of *divide-and-conquer*, is just as effective in our current societies, as at any point in human history. What is characteristic of our period, is the extent to which divide-and-conquer is a flagrantly *subversive* strategy delivered via mediums (media) that on the surface, profess to be something else. This means we live in a world where appearances are deceptive, and where the ideological functions are embedded quietly under a false pretense: whether that be the mainstream media as 'news', a T.V. show as 'entertainment', or an article as 'information'. 'It is just a T.V. show', 'it is just a movie', 'it is just a song'; are not uncommon expressions to hear from those who are otherwise totally ignorant of how ideology works, or otherwise have no interest (since they are under a form of ideological bondage, and have no way and no will to see outside of this).

We also discussed how these media functions will accelerate their role as ideological functions to an extreme, with the peak of the liberalist-globalist system and its subsequent decline. Because this 'peak' occurred before the system had fully consolidated and cemented its power, there is a kind of panic and desperation in the mobilization of the system to defend and reconsolidate itself. This makes it clumsy: and because it fails to understand that it is now, contrary to its own assumptions, 'on the wrong side of history'; its actions only further accelerate its own decline (and it enters into a form of *deep irrationality*). The more it loses traction, and furthers its own decline, the harder it tries to rescue itself. This means, 1: it exposes itself for what it is - as an ideological mechanism (and the media functions expose themselves), and 2: it further accelerates its own decline to the point of non-sustainability. At some point (in reaching the point of non-sustainability), it is has to resort to extreme measures, and fall back on its most powerful tools - exploited to an extreme degree - to rescue what power it has, and prevent the loss of more. In the case of media entities more broadly, these tools (or methods) are trauma strategies, optics constructs, paralysis strategies, mass censorship and victim narratives[107].

With victim narratives, this does not so much mean building new narratives (since the narratives have largely been built); but rather a case of activating, or triggering, those groups, or demographics (political and ideological *cells*), that they have already quietly engineered over time: just through delivering the right 'information' to these groups (narratives abstracted from any real context). In the case of trauma and paralysis, the news media now work towards absolute maximum fear, trauma and paralysis; because they understand well enough the crippling power of these things. The objective is to wear the populations down with so much perpetual fear and trauma, that 1: they are individually and collectively broken down - and in seeking respite and peace, will give the 'system' what it wants; and 2: they will transfer the tremendous frustration and animosity that comes with trauma, to the target that the *media* is

---

[107] One of the most successful functions this system has built, is the function of making organized opposition against it extremely difficult. It understands that by paralyzing oppositional forces and energy, and through fragmenting oppositional unity - even when it is on the back foot - it still has an upper hand. Difficult is not impossible however, and there are strategies that are effective against this 'system' (and increasingly so). Its optics, paralysis and fear structures, have been very useful in making functional opposition and organization difficult. Just the amount of effort it has to go to in order to maintain and reconsolidate power though, indicates how weak this system has become; and how effective an oppositional 'virus' has been in weakening it.

directing them toward. This means that apart from political groups, parties and figures; individuals and ideological groups will transfer their trauma, and direct their frustration and animosity toward: *other demographic groups* (and this is just what they are supposed to do and were engineered toward). This is the divide-and-conquer strategy in operation; and the news media, along with the 'system' at large, encourages, engineers and incentivizes *tribalism* and *factionalism*: whilst at the same time acting and pretending like tribalism and factionalism are (morally) wrong. This is part of the *moral role-play* that the media engage in, and just part of the larger 'optics' game it has become proficient at. Even though optics constructs are less effective than they used to be, and have lost much their power; the mass mobilization of an optics strategy can still be extremely effective. Optics games also have the effect of paralysis: not just paralyzing the relevant political figures or parties when needed; but also creating a paralysis amongst the populations in general - so that by and large - individuals are too demoralized and afraid to formulate meaningful opposition even if they want to. Optics games also come saturated with 'morality tales' and hand-wringing moral prostration; and in the more advanced stages of ideological warfare, will be a tool heavily relied upon by the system and its agents.

Our objective in *Part 2* of this book, will be to continue exploring the 'system' and its structures (as ideological functions): although apart from this task, we also want to place our political and ideological predicament within an even broader picture. It is quite apparent that a lot of ideological, cultural, economic and political significance, is attached to the United States of America, and the events that occur there. There is a very good reason for this, and this is largely to do with the philosophy that created the United States in the first place (and fact that the USA is a young, Western political system, uniquely founded on a democratic basis (as a Constitutional Republic))[108]. The American Project - America as a philosophical and political idea that broke from previous political and governmental structures - is largely of European origin (in the European Enlightenment); although of course, America developed and shaped its own destiny in a unique way. One reason why all eyes are on America, is because America was pitched as the promise of a new model of life and governance; that would set the standard for civilizations and governments throughout the world. It also became the world's largest super-power and a kind of empire in its own right: and ideas of a new hope and optimism attached to at least the *idea* of America, and an American future[109].

---

[108] As opposed to European nations for instance, that mostly have a much longer (ancient) political history and foundation.
[109] The 'American Dream' was an expression of this hope and optimism.

America is currently in a state of collapse however; and this collapse is severe (if not total), in that the political structures and functions of the United States, were severely jeopardized and subverted by groups and individuals hostile to the American project (or that wanted to transfer power away from the people and the government itself)[110]. The foundational principles of the United States are embedded in its Constitution; and this Constitution was supposed to be a kind of absolute and insurmountable basis for the protection of the nation going forward. It is a mistake to assume any foundational premise, moral premise, or political fundament, is immune to subversion and ambush; and the fate of the U.S. Constitution is testament to this fact. The promise of unity was also central to the American idea, its sustainability and prosperity. Division engineering has been a near total success in the United States, and, along with other factors, has devastated the principle of unity that was central to its foundational concept[111]. Because

---

[110] I.e. Into 'intelligence agencies', the military, trans-national and other non-governmental structures. This subversive element was both internal and external, and the internal elements were largely the most effective. As we stated earlier; it is certainly true that the American globalism that was engineered and formulated by certain groups and individuals with the advent of WW1 (and even prior to this), was largely formative in collapsing America in the long run. This is because the globalist trans-nationalist power structures (and 'intelligence' and military structures); although initially used for American global and financial dominance - eventually ended up paralyzing the American political structures and its independence.

[111] Even on U.S. currency, the Great Seal with its 'E pluribus unum' ('out of many, one'), is a testament to this principle of national unity

this division cannot be resolved 'diplomatically', or even democratically; this raises significant questions about the fate and future of 'democracy': not only in the U.S., but across the world more generally.

These arguments will be developed in more detail in *Part 2*, but they will centre around the fact of a constitutional crisis in America, and a crisis in *democracy* more generally[112]. Understanding the nature and reality of ideological division, brings to light many of the internal tensions and problems in the idea of democracy as such. We forget that democratic systems evolved within structures of greater ideological coherence and unity (and greater ethnic and cultural unity), than we have now. We must also remember that democracies, wherever they exist, are riddled with corrupting elements (and non-democratic elements) that practically render them non-democracies to begin with. Modern democracy, and the ambition to build democracies,

---

and coherence. It is also not uncommon to hear phrases like 'what unites us is stronger than what divides us'; although the reverse of this is more likely to be true (at least this is our current reality).

[112] It is not uncommon to hear pundits - or more academic media figures - talk about a 'crisis' in democracy; or some similarly phrased idea. Typically, the analyses that follow this concept are of little value as analysis; and this is because these analyses themselves, are functions of ideological engineering and narrative building (and thereby bear no real relation to, or understanding of, ideological affairs and the fate of actual democracy). More often than not, the intent of these analyses is to strike a kind of fear and panic into the reader (trauma strategy), and make them side with liberalist-globalist ambitions, narratives and structures.

however, is still relatively young; and it is not inaccurate to think of our failures in this respect, as a kind of trial-and-error. America, right now, is in a serious trial-by-fire; and the sheer burn of this trial will, of necessity, have a defining quality. America, and the Western world more generally, now has to stare into the face of the globalist Leviathan it has successfully built, armed and enabled, and that has ultimately consumed it in the process.

Bibliography of Cited References

Arnold, Matthew. *Culture and Anarchy*. Edited by P. J. Keating. Penguin, Penguin Classics, 2015.

Knight Foundation. (2018). *Indicators of news media trust.* Retrieved from https://kf-site-production.s3.amazonaws.com/media_elements/files/00 0/000/216/KnightFoundation_Panel4_Trust_Indicators_FI NAL.pdf

Nietzsche, Friedrich. *The Birth of Tragedy*. Translated by Shaun Whiteside, Edited by Michael Tanner. Penguin, Penguin Classics. 1993.

Zucker reference: https://variety.com/2016/tv/news/jeff-zucker-cnn-fox-news-1201827824/